LITERACY ESSENTIALS

Jenny Thomas, Diane White
and Kathryn Ryan

Literacy Essentials
1st Edition
Jenny Thomas
Diane White
Kathryn Ryan

Cover designer: Cheryl Smith, Macarn Design
Text designer: Cheryl Smith, Macarn Design
Production controller: Chantelle Bryant

Acknowledgements
The authors and publisher wish to thank the following people and organisations for permission to use the resources in this textbook. Page 10: Extract from *The Reluctant Hero* courtesy of Willie Apiata and Penguin Random House NZ. Page 12: *Ride like your aunty is watching* courtesy of Metlink and the Greater Wellington Regional Council, illustrations by Mary Guo. Page 14: The Underwater Classroom courtesy of *Dive New Zealand* and *DivePacific*. Page 16: Extract from *A Portrait of New Zealand* courtesy by Warren Jacobs and Robin Smith, text by Errol Braithwaite, 1999 edition (since substantially revised). Thanks also to Upstart Press. Page 20: Extract from *Keeping Promises: The Treaty Settlement Processes*, School Journal Level 4 November 2017 courtesy of Ministry of Education. Page 22: Extract from *Mussel Building* by Kate Evans courtesy of *New Zealand Geographic*. Page 24: Extract from *Cook Strait curse strikes again* by Tom Hunt, courtesy of *Marlborough Midweek* and Stuff Limited. Page 26: *Chatham honey tours* courtesy of The New Zealand Beekeeper. Page 30: *School embraces RecycleKiwi* courtesy of CrestCean. Page 32: Advertisement courtesy of Polished Diamonds Jewellery Design. Page 34: *Kura Māori empowering next generation*, courtesy of *The Education Gazette/Tukutuku Koreo*. Page 36: *A career highlight* courtesy of Lynette McFadden. Page 38: Extract from *Science of the Ice*, School Journal Level 4 November 2018 courtesy of the Ministry of Education. Page 40: Extract from *Wildboy: The Journey of Brando Yelavich*, by Stephanie Chamberlin, School Journal Level 4 May 2016 courtesy of Ministry of Education.

For product information and technology assistance,
in Australia call **1300 790 853**;
in New Zealand call **0800 449 725**

For permission to use material from this text or product, please email
aust.permissions@cengage.com

National Library of New Zealand Cataloguing-in-Publication Data
A catalogue record for this book is available from the National Library of New Zealand.

978 0 17 047758 1

Cengage Learning Australia
Level 5, 80 Dorcas Street
Southbank VIC 3006 Australia

Printed in China by 1010 Printing International Limited.
7 27 26 25

CONTENTS

Welcome to Literacy

To achieve an NCEA qualification, you need to show that you are **literate**. This means that you are able to use and understand language in a range of day-to-day situations.

- You need to show that you can **read** language in many forms (i.e. articles, books, messages, texts and images) and **understand what you read**.
- You need to show that you can **write** in different forms, reasonably accurately, to express your thoughts and ideas clearly for a particular purpose.

If you are using English as the language to show your literacy, you need to pass two specific Unit Standards. These are called co-requisites:

1 *Unit Standard 32403* — 5 credits
Demonstrate understanding of ideas and information in written texts.

and

2 *Unit Standard 32405* — 5 credits
Write texts to communicate ideas and information.

What is literacy?

Literacy is:

- **Reading** to understand.

You read: non-fiction books, fiction books, internet items, magazine articles, manga, graphic novels, TV screen ads, newspaper articles, poetry, instruction manuals, weather reports, emails, text messages, … all the time.

- **Writing** to express thoughts and ideas.

You write: for school study in *all* subjects, letters, emails, text messages, notes, job sheets, … all the time.

You will need to develop this skill of literacy to get on with your life after you leave school, whichever way you go. These two Literacy assessments are **part of achieving NCEA** and you can sit the Common Assessment Activity (CAA) from Year 9 onwards. This assessment is digital and your school will organise it for you when you are ready. The reading and writing standards will each take about an hour to complete, but there is no time limit on the assessment.

ISBN: 9780170477581

Let's get reading
Kia pānui tātou

In the Literacy Reading assessment (US 32403), you will be expected to:

- read a range of written texts of different types and varying lengths

and

- answer questions to show that you can read and understand ideas and information.

These questions will likely take the form of multiple-choice questions, but may also include other types of questions such as matching and labelling.

The texts

In the Literacy Reading assessment, the texts will be selected from things you might read or experience in everyday life. You may be given a text from a newspaper or a school journal, a non-fiction book or an internet post. The text may be a series of social media messages or emails.

- There will be at least four texts to be read in the assessment.
- At least one of the texts will be more than 200 words.
- There will be a combination of continuous text (for example essays, chapters or books) and non-continuous text (for example lists, tables, charts, graphs, images and pānui supported by a significant element of written information).

The questions

In the Literacy Reading assessment, the questions will likely be **multiple choice**, as this is the format of the assessment so far. However, there may be other types of questions.

In this workbook, we have decided to include short-answer questions on the first 10 texts. These are included to get you thinking more deeply about the text and will help when you have to close read text in other subjects.

These short-answer questions will check that you have read the text by asking:

> **on-the-surface questions**, where the answers are right there in front of you, written in the text, and you just need to locate them
>
> and
>
> **below-the-surface questions**, which will check your understanding by asking you questions about words and what they mean, about the author's purpose and reliability, and also about what the main ideas of the texts are. These questions will require you to think more deeply and also read between the lines (looking for what is hinted at, but not said outright).

Are you a good reader?

A good reader is an active reader who typically does the following things:

- Pays attention to the **title**: usually the title is informative.
- **Scans** around the text for information about the writer, the date of publication or where the information has come from.
- **Skims** the piece: looks quickly at a text to get a basic idea of the content and main points. Uses headlines and images to help them gain an overall understanding when skimming.
- **Scans** the text: looks for specific information (linked to the reader's purpose) by quickly scanning for key words and/or phrases.
- **Annotates**: jots down thoughts and highlights things that stand out. In the assessment, there is a function that allows you to make notes on a little square, like a digital sticky note.
- **Infers**: uses clues from the text and prior knowledge to draw conclusions about why the text has been written.

Don't worry, you do most of these things automatically when you read.

This workbook will give you lots of opportunities to practise these reading techniques in preparation for the Literacy Reading assessment.

Seeing is believing

Let's look at a sample text and how to find the answers to multiple-choice questions.

Read the text

You should **read the text** through once in its entirety (this means the whole thing including the title and any other source/publication details that are provided). Read through the text below before we go any further.

National Honey Competition

New Zealand's premier honey competition will be judged by a panel of internationally trained judges across 12 categories to find the country's best products.

As well as showcasing honey, the National Honey Competition is an opportunity to present other products of the hive such as beeswax, pollen or propolis, as well as honey beverages and product packaging. The judges are keen to see more entries in these categories to demonstrate the innovation and creativity currently going on within the industry.

All honey producers are invited to enter. Full details of the competition, class categories and how to enter can be found on the ApiNZ website.

ISBN: 9780170477581

On-the-surface questions

Now let's look at a multiple-choice question that asks you an *on-the-surface* question.

1 Who will be **judging** the National Honey Competition?

The key word here is **judging**. You want to use your *scanning* skills to quickly scan the text for the word **judging**/**judge**/ **judged**/**judges**.

Found it? Now look for the answer from the multiple-choice list below:

TIP: If one of the possible answers doesn't match up with where you saw the word you are scanning for, then keep reading. It is possible that the word is mentioned twice, and the answer is further down the text.

- (A) Local honey producers
- (B) A panel of internationally trained judges
- (C) The ApiNZ website
- (D) Beekeeping enthusiasts

Remember, this is an ***on-the-surface*** question, so the answer is right there, in the text, waiting to be found.

Check the answers to see if you got it correct!

Below-the-surface questions

Next, let's look at how to answer a *below-the-surface* multiple-choice question. You will need to re-read the relevant part/s of the text and think about what the text is saying in relation to the question. Here is an example:

2 What is the purpose of including products other than honey in the National Honey Competition?

The key words here are **'What is the purpose of …'**. Remember, this is a *below-the-surface* question, so you will need to dive a bit between the lines of the text to find the correct answer.

Let's look at the possible answers we have been provided:

TIP: Remember that the answer is there, hidden in the options. Sometimes, you might not know the right answer straight away, but through eliminating the **wrong** answers, you can narrow down your options and then the correct one will become clear.

- (A) To showcase the versatility of honeybees and their products.
- (B) To encourage participants to diversify their production.
- (C) To reduce the environmental impact of beekeeping.
- (D) To increase the amount of products sold in the market.

All of these answers suggest a possible purpose for including products other than honey. This makes sense as this is a below-the-surface question, we have to dive deeper and think more to figure out what the correct answer is.

ISBN: 9780170477581

Next, go back to the part of the text that mentions the other products being included and re-read that, looking for key words from the suggested answers such as **versatility**, **diversity**, **environmental**, **sold** and **market** or similar. We have pulled out the relevant section below to help.

> *As well as showcasing honey, the National Honey Competition is an opportunity to present other products of the hive such as beeswax, pollen or propolis, as well as honey beverages and product packaging. The judges are keen to see more entries in these categories to demonstrate the innovation and creativity currently going on within the industry.*

TIP: The answer may not be in the first part of the text, so you need to know what key words you are scanning for when you look through the text. You may need to scan much or even most of the text to find the answer; this is okay!

Immediately, we can eliminate **C** and **D** as options because there is no mention of environmental impact or selling in the market.

- (A) To showcase the versatility of honeybees and their products.
- (B) To encourage participants to diversify their production.
- ~~(C) To reduce the environmental impact of beekeeping.~~
- ~~(D) To increase the amount of products sold in the market.~~

That leaves us with **A** or **B** as the most likely answers. Read through the section of text another time. Remember, the question is asking you about **purpose**. There is a key line in the text which states 'The judges are keen to see …' — see it? Read it and make a decision between **A** and **B** from the information you are given.

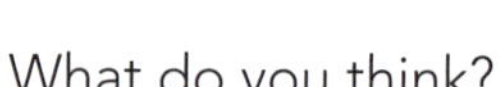

What do you think?

Circle  

Justify your choice:

____

____

You can check your final answer in the back of the book.

ISBN: 9780170477581

Building on your skills

Remember, in the Reading assessment, the questions you will answer will likely be a variety of multiple-choice questions but may also include other types of questions such as labelling and matching. However, for the first set of practice texts in this book, we have included short-answer questions. It is important to answer the short-answer questions because they are designed to help you improve your understanding of the ideas and information in a text. Practising these skills will help you become faster in finding the answers to the questions when you are in the assessment.

Finally

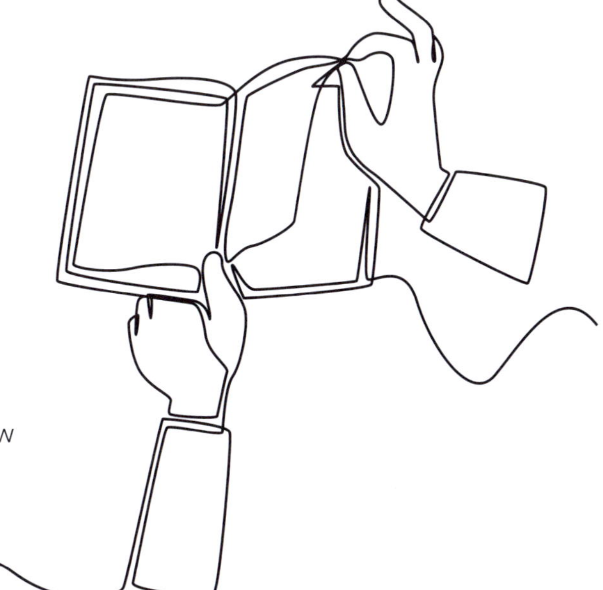

We can all read. We all do read.

Every day, every time you open your phone, you are reading. But we are not all readers. We don't all read for enjoyment, and that's okay. But what we all **do** need to do is read for **understanding**.

We live in an increasingly digital age. We are bombarded with words that want to influence how we behave, how we dress, how we spend our money, how we think. We need to understand **what** we read, to know **who** wrote the words, to know **why** the words have been written.

If you **read with understanding**, you will navigate the digital age with confidence.

Having worked through this section of the book, you are ready to start practising for the Literacy Reading assessment beginning on the next page.

ISBN: 9780170477581

Text 1: Tracking from *The Reluctant Hero*

Read the extract below adapted from *The Reluctant Hero* and answer the questions that follow. In this extract, Victoria Cross recipient Willie Apiata discusses his experience of being on a tracking course.

Tracking is tuning in to what's around you. It's a lot like hunting. When you come across signs of a pig, like its footprints, first you judge its size, then the age, how many pigs there are, and where they are heading. The footprints may be **fresh** or getting old. You might find **faeces** that's still warm. And if you know the area well because you have hunted there before, you can work out more than that. A tracker can see things where someone who isn't trained could be looking for ages and never see anything. **And they can tell a whole story from it.**

In a way, good tracking is the combination of a lot of skills people don't realise they already have. Take a field on a frosty morning — if someone has walked across it, you can tell things like which way they are going from the colour of the grass. Where the grass has been flattened, the colour will be dull, because it has been walked on. The way the grass is pointing tells you which way the person is walking.

We learnt about covering tracks, too. In the snow, you brush over where you've walked. And in the bush, when you've walked through a place and pushed the grass over, you turn around and push it back the other way after you've gone through. **It's like opening and closing a gate** — although sometimes you can leave more signs trying to cover your tracks than you made in the first place.

Our main purpose on the exercise was to lay tracks and leave footprints for the trainers to find and follow in the bush. We would go half a day or a day ahead, and they had to work out where we were heading, how many of us there were and gather as much information from our tracks as they could.

We got to sit in on the presentation at the end of the course and we saw how much information they had gathered. It was incredible. For instance, they knew I was the gunner in the group because they picked up how my gun was always resting, and that, because we were on the run, I was always watching the rear. And because it was my first time doing anything like this, I'd been stubbing my cigarettes out in the ground and hiding them as we went along, but they saw the **indentations**. In the presentation, they produced a plastic bag full of my cigarette butts. I couldn't believe it.

Select (✓) the correct answer to the multiple-choice questions below. It is best practice to re-read the text to find the correct answer.

1 What is tracking a lot like?

- (A) hunting
- (B) boating
- (C) skiing
- (D) orienteering

2 '***It's like opening and closing a gate …***' means what in the context of this piece?

- (A) That Apiata opened and closed a gate.
- (B) That it's a clear process.
- (C) To work on a farm.
- (D) To cover your tracks.

ISBN: 9780170477581

3 Why couldn't Apiata believe it when they produced a plastic bag full of his cigarette butts?

(A) He didn't think they would pick them up.
(B) He thought he had hidden them really well.
(C) He didn't think they were relevant to the tracking.
(D) He didn't realise he smoked that much.

4 *'… I'd been stubbing my cigarettes out in the ground and hiding them as we went along, but they saw the **indentations**.'*

What would be the best definition of 'indentation' as it is used in the text?

(A) A bulge on the edge or surface of something.
(B) A notch or hole on the edge or surface of something.
(C) A gap between two planks.
(D) A bump in the dirt.

5 *'The footprints may be **fresh** or getting old.'*

Which word could best replace 'fresh' in this sentence?

(A) crisp
(B) raw
(C) youthful
(D) recent

Short-answer questions

We have included short-answer questions here, as they will help you develop your skills in reading texts and understanding the ideas and information that is being presented to you. Practising these skills will help you become faster in finding the answers to the questions when you are in the assessment.

6 Tracking is like hunting. Which audience is Apiata aiming at by using this comparison?

____

____

7 What is the risk, Apiata says, you take when trying to cover your tracks?

____

____

8 What does the phrase '***And they can tell a whole story from it.***' mean?

____

____

9 Why did Apiata use the word 'faeces' in the sentence *'You might find **faeces** that's still warm.'* rather than 'poo'?

____

____

10 Apiata says good tracking is the combination of a lot of skills people don't realise they already have. What sort of skills do you think we have that could be useful?

____

____

ISBN: 9780170477581

Text 2: Ride like your aunty is watching

Read the extract below from *Metlink.org.nz* and answer the questions that follow.

A Metlink campaign aiming to create more pleasant journeys for customers and frontline staff by reminding passengers of onboard etiquette is being rolled out across its network.

Metlink General Manager Samantha Gain says its launch is well timed with Metlink's two largest operators making significant progress on recruiting new drivers through individual recruitment campaigns and newly opened pathways for immigration.

Alongside thanking onboard staff and drivers, with COVID still around the campaign also encourages good hygiene habits, creating space for others and giving up priority seats among other messages.

Each message was devised alongside operators and using passenger feedback from Metlink's complaints database.

The instruction to 'Ride like your aunty is watching' features on each concept and is drawn from insight that good behaviour is exhibited when a senior family member is around.

"We want people to smile when they see the illustrations and take a moment to think about others on their journey. With its **relatable tone** and clever illustrations, we're confident the messages will be well received," adds Ms Gain.

Metlink's **'customer etiquette' information campaign** initially began in 2020 but was disrupted for two years due to COVID. It cost $176,000 over three years, including design, production and installation across nearly 200 train carriages, over 450 buses, and three harbour ferries.

Select (✓) the correct answer to the multiple-choice questions below. It is best practice to re-read the text to find the correct answer.

1 What is the best word to replace 'etiquette' in this sentence?

*'Metlink's "customer **etiquette**" information campaign initially began in 2020 but was disrupted for two years due to COVID.'*

- (A) good manners
- (B) rules
- (C) conduct
- (D) actions

2 What type of word is **Metlink**?

- (A) verb
- (B) adjective
- (C) proper noun
- (D) noun

 ISBN: 9780170477581

3 What is the *'Ride like your aunty is watching'* concept based on?

- (A) That everyone has an aunty.
- (B) That if a senior member of your family is around, you will behave better.
- (C) Surveillance.
- (D) Getting you to smile.

4 What was the main delay in getting the '***"customer etiquette" information campaign***' off the ground?

- (A) cost
- (B) long process
- (C) consulting the community
- (D) COVID

5 Which of the images are targeted at teenagers?

- (A) A + B
- (B) B + C
- (C) C + D
- (D) B + D

Short-answer questions

We have included short-answer questions here, as they will help you develop your skills in reading texts and understanding the ideas and information that is being presented to you. Practising these skills will help you become faster in finding the answers to the questions when you are in the assessment.

6 What does Ms Gain mean when she says the illustrations have a '***relatable tone***'?

____

____

7 What is Metlink and what does it do?

____

____

8 This information was published on the Metlink website under More Information → Getting Started → Maps, apps & guides → Customer etiquette. Who would be the target audience for this article?

____

____

9 Who else apart from teenagers are targeted in this campaign? Are the topics it covers important?

____

____

10 Explain your answer to question **5**.

____

____

Text 3: The Underwater Classroom

Read the extract below adapted from *Dive New Zealand* and answer the questions that follow.

We are students in our second year of being part of the Experiencing Marine Reserves (EMR) marine education programme. EMR is learning about the ocean, its biodiversity, and the animals'/plants' adaptations to different habitats.

We decided to go to Wellington to check out two of their marine reserves: Taputeranga and Kāpiti Island. We wanted to see how biodiversity changes in different types of places …

Finally it was the big day. We headed in convoy to Wellington with 32 students and 18 adults. On arrival we went to the Red Rocks for coastline exploration. It was interesting to see the different seaweeds including huge bull kelp and we saw New Zealand fur seals sunbathing on the rocks.

On our second day the sea was rough so we explored **Baithouse Aquarium**. It had a small touch tank with starfish, triplefins, kina, hermit crabs and more. We were lucky to see the aquarium at night which gave us the chance to see how animals behave differently at different times.

The next afternoon we had our first snorkel at Kao Bay. We were amazed by our first view of giant kelp forests **and were careful not to become tangled or panic**. For some it was our first experience of snorkelling in the sea and it was very successful.

Our last day was at Kāpiti Island. We were excited and some were nervous. One group explored the island while the other snorkelled. **There were moon jellyfish everywhere but we soon discovered they don't sting**. We saw a lot of fish we hadn't seen at Kao Bay. **Sitting on and amongst the rocks like marine couch potatoes were sea cucumbers.** Paua were scattered over the rocks like barnacles on a whale.

The trip was lots of fun and a great learning experience. We learnt about the differences in biodiversity between Cook Strait and Goat Island. The Underwater Classroom provided a good personal experience of the differences between areas and habitats. We learnt more in a short time through actual experiences than using books and the internet.

Select (✓) the correct answer to the multiple-choice questions below. It is best practice to re-read the text to find the correct answer.

1 Skim the passage for the initials EMR. What do they stand for?

- (A) Enriching Marine Reserves
- (B) Encourage Marine Rescue
- (C) Enjoying Marine Resources
- (D) Experiencing Marine Reserves

2 *'On our second day the sea was rough so we explored* ***Baithouse Aquarium****.'*

Why does 'Baithouse Aquarium' have capital letters?

- (A) Because it is the name of a business (proper noun).
- (B) Because it is a doing word (verb).
- (C) Because it is a describing word (adjective).
- (D) Because it is the name of something (noun).

ISBN: 9780170477581

3 ***'... and were careful not to become tangled or panic.'***

What is the main reason the author uses this phrase?

- (A) To describe what it is like underwater.
- (B) To explain that it can be dangerous underwater.
- (C) To show they love the sea.
- (D) To show they worked hard to get here.

4 Why has the sentence '***Sitting on and amongst the rocks like marine couch potatoes were sea cucumbers.***' been used?

- (A) To compare the sea cucumbers to potatoes.
- (B) To show us how active sea cucumbers are.
- (C) To help us understand that the sea cucumbers don't move much.
- (D) Because the sea cucumbers are lazy.

5 The author feels that experiences outside of the school classroom are:

- (A) worthwhile and enriching.
- (B) difficult and time consuming.
- (C) enjoyable and a good change.
- (D) a lot of work.

Short-answer questions

We have included short-answer questions here, as they will help you develop your skills in reading texts and understanding the ideas and information that is being presented to you. Practising these skills will help you become faster in finding the answers to the questions when you are in the assessment.

6 Scan the sentences before and after when EMR appears in the text. Describe in your own words what the purpose of EMR is.

____

____

7 Re-read paragraph 4. Why were the students lucky to be there at night?

____

____

8 Re-read paragraph 5. What could possibly happen if the students '***become tangled or panic***'?

____

____

9 The sentence '***There were moon jellyfish everywhere but we soon discovered they don't sting.***' implies that ...

____

____

10 Find a quote from the text that reinforces your answer for question **5**.

____

____

Text 4: North Island: A Volcanic Heritage

Read the extract below from the introduction to *A Portrait of New Zealand* and answer the questions that follow.

North Island: A Volcanic Heritage

According to Māori tradition the North Island of New Zealand was a fish, caught by the demi-god Māui. The canoe from which he caught this fish became the South Island, with Stewart Island as its anchor stone. This story sets the North Island atmosphere perfectly, because the hauling up of a fish of such a prodigious size is suggestive of Homeric spectacle — and the North Island is **spectacular**. It also suggests mystery, because how a people who knew no maps managed to perceive the fish-like shape of an island some 1000km (620 miles) long is a mystery, the answer to which is buried deep in Māori lore.

The tale goes on to tell how Māui's brothers, half-crazed with hunger, leaped onto the monstrous fish and began to devour it raw, so that it is gouged and scarred, and its backbone exposed; and the picture thus conjured up is indeed **a fair enough depiction of the North Island's highlands**.

Visitors to New Zealand, coming first to the North Island, sometimes express surprise at the fact that they see no high alps and no mighty glaciers, though such features often fill New Zealand's commercial travel literature almost to the exclusion of all else. Yet few such comments reveal any sense of disappointment. On the contrary, the ecstatic visitor usually finds fresh evidence each day that what the North Island lacks in scenic grandeur, it makes up for in sheer spectacle.

For this is a land in which the creative forces of nature are still awesomely at work. The same applies in the South Island; but where the Southern Alps have been pushed up gradually, over aeons of time, by the infinitely ponderous movement of the plates of the earth's fractured crust, the highest mountains of the North Island have often leaped into being, or have suddenly disappeared, sometimes within remembered history, as the result or aftermath of violent (volcanic) explosions.

The force which shaped this landscape, which collapsed it, tossed it, tumbled and tangled it, is still there, still visible, still working, still smoking and steaming and filling the air with its sulphurous breath.

Select (✓) the correct answer to the multiple-choice questions below. It is best practice to re-read the text to find the correct answer.

1 What do visitors to New Zealand, starting in the North Island, often express surprise at?

- (A) The amount of farmland.
- (B) The volcanic activity.
- (C) The lack of alps and glaciers.
- (D) How it is in the shape of a fish.

2 What is the best word to replace 'spectacular' in the sentence '*… and the North Island is **spectacular**.*'?

- (A) miraculous
- (B) magnificent
- (C) theatrical
- (D) staggering

 ISBN: 9780170477581

3 Why does this introduction to the North Island mention Māui, a demi-god from Māori pūrākau (storytelling)?

(A) Because it is a great tale.
(B) Because he is relevant to the topic.
(C) To show an understanding and appreciation of the culture of the native people of New Zealand.
(D) All of the above.

4 What is the author's attitude towards the North Island?

(A) indifferent
(B) positive
(C) negative
(D) disappointed

5 What does the author state is the main difference between the North and South Island?

(A) The shape
(B) The size
(C) The people
(D) The speed at which the landscape was created

Short-answer questions

We have included short-answer questions here, as they will help you develop your skills in reading texts and understanding the ideas and information that is being presented to you. Practising these skills will help you become faster in finding the answers to the questions when you are in the assessment.

6 Explain why the image of Māui's brothers devouring the fish raw is '***… a fair enough depiction of the North Island's highlands***'.

____

____

7 How does the title of the piece link to the body of the piece?

____

____

8 Find three adjectives or adverbs from the piece that prove your answer to question **4**.

____

____

9 What is '***The force which shaped this landscape***' and how do you know?

____

____

10 What does the author think is mysterious about the idea that the North Island was a fish?

____

____

ISBN: 9780170477581

Text 5: Reviews of the novel *The Bone Tiki*

Read the reviews below and answer the questions that follow.

The Bone Tiki by David Hair is an awesome adventure story that had me hooked from start to finish. It put together mythology and modern-day action which I liked a lot. I understood why the characters did what they did and the plot is full of twists and turns. A must-read for any teen who loves a good adventure!
— Ramesh

Are you looking for a novel set in New Zealand that mixes mythology and modern adventure and **captivates readers** from start to finish? Then *The Bone Tiki* is for you! David Hair's amazing use of Māori culture and legends adds a depth to the story that's hard to find in other books. As the main character says, I also 'learned things about my own culture I didn't even know,' making this book not only a thrilling read, but also an educational one. *The Bone Tiki* is a must-read for any New Zealand teenager looking for an adventure story.
— **Vanessa**

The Bone Tiki by David Hair was fascinating in some ways, especially the way it shows Māori mythology. The plot is full of action and suspense, but I couldn't connect with the main character, Mat. He came across as selfish and reckless, and I found myself wanting to know more about the other characters instead. Despite this, the book is interesting and I would recommend it to anyone looking for action and suspense in a New Zealand setting.
— **Ben**

The Bone Tiki by David Hair is a New Zealand book that offers a blend of adventure and Māori mythology. While I found the **pacing** a bit slow at times, the story is well-written and engaging, and the cultural references add a fresh take to the typical adventure plot. Overall, it's a tolerable book written for the YA reader, that's worth checking out if you're a fan of the genre.
— **Mei**

The Bone Tiki by David Hair puts Māori mythology alongside modern life adventure but I was disappointed with its ending. The book built up to an exciting climax, but the way it finished felt rushed and unsatisfying. As the main character says: "I was left with nothing but questions." However, it is easy to read and the Māori mythology adds an interesting layer to the plot. **I think it is worth a read for the journey, even if the destination falls short.**
— **Chris**

Select (✓) the correct answer to the multiple-choice questions below. It is best practice to re-read the text to find the correct answer.

1 '***I think it is worth a read for the journey, even if the destination falls short.***' means that Chris thought the book

- (A) was fabulous.
- (B) was exciting.
- (C) had a good conclusion.
- (D) was disappointing in the end.

2 The reviewer who tells you the most about the characters is:

- (A) Mei.
- (B) Ben.
- (C) Vanessa.
- (D) Ramesh.

ISBN: 9780170477581

3 Many reviews are written as if they are a conversation between the writer and reader. The best example of this is the review written by

(A) Ramesh.
(B) Mei.
(C) Chris.
(D) Vanessa.

4 Which of these reviewers seemed to like the book the best?

(A) Ramesh
(B) Chris
(C) Ben
(D) Mei

5 Who is most likely to be a professional book critic?

(A) Mei
(B) Ben
(C) Chris
(D) Vanessa

Short-answer questions

We have included short-answer questions here, as they will help you develop your skills in reading texts and understanding the ideas and information that is being presented to you. Practising these skills will help you become faster in finding the answers to the questions when you are in the assessment.

6 Which reviewer is likely a 'bot' and what clues are there to this?

____

____

7 *'Are you looking for a novel set in New Zealand that blends mythology and modern adventure and **captivates readers** from start to finish?'*

Suggest a word or phrase to replace 'captivates readers'.

____

____

8 How do we know that Vanessa is likely a New Zealander?

____

____

9 What does Mei mean when she uses the word '**pacing**'?

____

____

10 Most of the reviewers use a lot of descriptive language, for example *amazing, thrilling, fascinating, awesome, engaging, exciting, captivates*. What makes this genre (reviews) suitable for this type of language?

____

____

Text 6: Settlement Opinion

Read the extracts below from the article *Keeping Promises: The Treaty Settlement Process* by Mark Darby and answer the questions that follow.

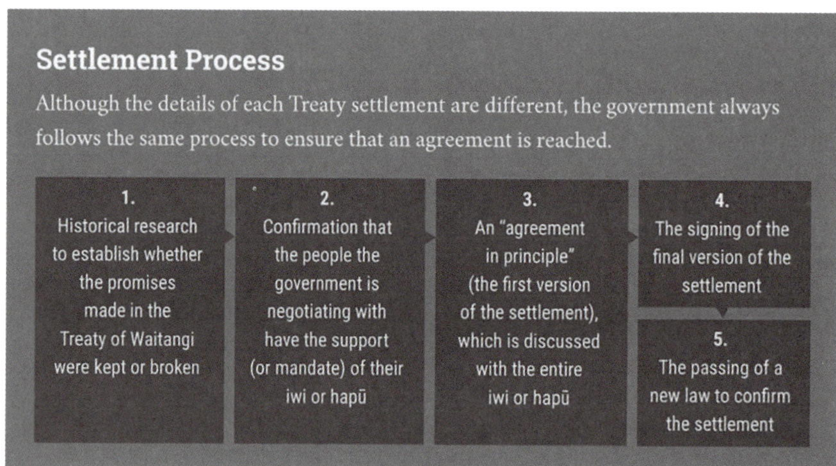

Settlement Process

Although the details of each Treaty settlement are different, the government always follows the same process to ensure that an agreement is reached.

1. Historical research to establish whether the promises made in the Treaty of Waitangi were kept or broken
2. Confirmation that the people the government is negotiating with have the support (or mandate) of their iwi or hapū
3. An "agreement in principle" (the first version of the settlement), which is discussed with the entire iwi or hapū
4. The signing of the final version of the settlement
5. The passing of a new law to confirm the settlement

SETTLEMENT OPINION

TENETI RIRINUI

(Ngāti Te Rangi)

My whānau are from Tauranga. I wasn't involved in our Treaty settlement process but followed it closely. Because of the courage and mahi of my wider whānau, I learnt a lot about our past. Their research and submissions taught me how historical events shaped where we are today. Although our settlement deed marks the official end of the process, the real challenge lies in how we use the experience to meet the aspirations of our people.

MATAHANA TIKAO CALMAN

(Kāi Tahu, Ngāti Raukawa, Ngāti Toa)

I think the Treaty settlement process has been a positive step for Māori, especially the hope it's given for the future of te reo Māori. Kāi Tahu have greatly benefited, being one of the first iwi to settle. It's meant I've received help to pay for tutoring. A Treaty settlement also means I can apply for Kāi Tahu scholarships to study at university.

REREMOANA WALKER

(Ngāti Porou)

I grieve when I hear Pākehā landowners proudly talking about the land they inherited from their fathers and grandfathers when it was once Māori land – watch *Country Calendar*! The Waitangi Tribunal has recognised these injustices, but wise heads are now needed so that iwi can manage these funds to benefit all Māori in their rohe.

TERENCE TAMAKEHU

(Te Āti Haunui-a-Pāpārangi)

I live in South Taranaki, where pretty much everything was taken from Māori, whether they fought against the Crown or not. The government didn't care about the details. Land confiscation was just an excuse to take what it wanted. The Treaty settlement process hasn't affected me personally, but nothing can make up for what happened to Māori.

35

Select (✓) the correct answer to the multiple-choice questions below. It is best practice to re-read the text to find the correct answer.

1 What happens at the end of a settlement process?

- (A) The recipients get money.
- (B) There is historical research to see if the promises made in Te Tiriti o Waitangi | The Treaty of Waitangi were kept or broken.
- (C) The document is signed.
- (D) There is a passing of a new law to confirm the settlement.

2 How would you best describe the **tone** of Terence Tamakehu's opinion?

- (A) comforting
- (B) worried
- (C) excited
- (D) upset

ISBN: 9780170477581

3 What did Teneti Ririnui learn from the Treaty settlement process?

- (A) A lot about our past/how historical events shaped where we are today.
- (B) That it is a boring process.
- (C) That he needed to be involved to benefit.
- (D) That we need a strong economy.

4 Which word can best replace Teneti's word 'aspirations' in this sentence?

'*... how we use the experience to meet the **aspirations** of our people.*'

- (A) thoughts
- (B) ambitions
- (C) destinations
- (D) plans

5 Why does Reremoana Walker reference *Country Calendar*?

- (A) Because it is a well-known New Zealand television programme that talks about farming in New Zealand without acknowledging the original owners of the land.
- (B) Because he wants you to watch it.
- (C) Because he works for *Country Calendar*.
- (D) Because he thinks it should be cancelled.

Short-answer questions

We have included short-answer questions here, as they will help you develop your skills in reading texts and understanding the ideas and information that is being presented to you. Practising these skills will help you become faster in finding the answers to the questions when you are in the assessment.

6 Why are the details of each Treaty settlement different?

___

___

7 Do you think the authors of this piece have covered a wide enough range of people to get a broad picture of opinions on this topic? Why/why not?

___

___

8 Which opinion is the most positive and focused on an encouraging future? Justify your opinion.

___

___

9 Whose opinion is the most trustworthy and reliable out of the four? Justify your opinion.

___

___

10 What is the purpose of including an 'opinion' section after an article?

___

___

Text 7: Mussel Building

Read the extract below from *New Zealand Geographic* and answer the questions that follow.

MUSSEL BUILDING

WRITTEN BY **KATE EVANS**

ONE DAY IN 2008, marine science student Kura Paul-Burke was diving in Ōhiwa's murky waters when the grey-brown of the sea floor suddenly gave way to a **brilliant orange**. At first, she was struck by the beauty of it. Then she realised she was looking at hundreds of thousands of 11-armed sea stars—pātangaroa, a native species—stacked five or six layers deep. Behind them, the seabed was littered with empty green-lipped mussel shells.

In 2007, the Bay of Plenty harbour was home to an estimated 112 million mussels. By 2019, only 78,000 were left.

Paul-Burke's Ngāti Awa elders had noticed signs of decline well before then. No-one knew why the mussels were dying. Was it overharvesting? **Sedimentation**? But they knew there used to be more mussel beds, and in 2006, they urged her to investigate—then helped her **to map the old mussel beds using both traditional landmarks and scuba surveys**.

Researchers are still confirming the starfish are to blame, and figuring out what is causing the ecosystem imbalance in the harbour. In the meantime, Paul-Burke—now a professor of mātai moana (marine research) at the University of Waikato—wanted to see if it was possible to save the mussels and the harbour. The project wove together four iwi (Ngāti Awa, Te Ūpokorehe, Te Whakatōhea and Waimana Kaakū [Tūhoe]) and three councils, kaumātua and young people.

Together, they built four restoration stations where baby mussel spat could attach and grow. **Instead of using commercial plastic spat lines, they experimented with natural fibres**. The strongest were made from fallen tī kōuka leaves woven into rope by master weaver Rokahurihia Ngarimu-Cameron and her students. In late 2018, the team hung them on floats in midwater, out of the reach of clambering starfish.

It worked. Mussels began growing in such numbers that they dragged the floats under the surface. When the tī kōuka lines eventually degraded, young mussels fell to the bottom "as a whānau", Paul-Burke says, before reattaching to the sea floor.

As the researchers describe in a new paper, by 2021, three new mussel beds had formed close to the restoration stations, and the mussel population had increased ten-fold—showing what can be accomplished, says Paul-Burke, when several knowledge streams and communities pull together.

Select (✓) the correct answer to the multiple-choice questions below. It is best practice to re-read the text to find the correct answer.

1 What caused the sea floor to be a '***brilliant orange***'?

- (A) mussels
- (B) fish
- (C) sea stars
- (D) coral

2 *'No-one knew why the mussels were dying. Was it overharvesting? **Sedimentation**?'*

What is the best word to replace 'Sedimentation'?

- (A) Dislodging
- (B) Accumulation
- (C) Dirt
- (D) Overflow

ISBN: 9780170477581

3 Re-read paragraph 5 looking for the word '**spat**' — what does spat likely mean?

- (A) A method to collect baby mussels.
- (B) The shells of young mussels.
- (C) Small floating debris in the water.
- (D) Baby mussels that attach to rocks or ropes (lines) to grow.

4 What is the main thing the article is concerned with?

- (A) The decline of mussels in the Bay of Plenty harbour.
- (B) The quality of the water in the Bay of Plenty harbour.
- (C) Mapping the seabed of the Bay of Plenty harbour.
- (D) Making sure pātangaroa (11-armed sea stars) survive.

5 What is the overall take-away message from this article?

- (A) That mussels are dying.
- (B) That pātangaroa must be eradicated (wiped out).
- (C) That people from different areas need to work together.
- (D) That we should leave pātangaroa alone.

Short-answer questions

We have included short-answer questions here, as they will help you develop your skills in reading texts and understanding the ideas and information that is being presented to you. Practising these skills will help you become faster in finding the answers to the questions when you are in the assessment.

6 How do you know from the first paragraph that this article is about a place in Aotearoa New Zealand?

____

____

7 Why did the Ngāti Awa elders help Kura Paul-Burke '***to map the old mussel beds using both traditional landmarks and scuba surveys***'?

____

____

8 What is the likely connection between the decline of the mussels and the rise of the pātangaroa and how do we know this?

____

____

9 '***Instead of using commercial plastic spat lines, they experimented with natural fibres.***'

Why would the project team not look at plastic spat lines?

____

____

10 What has been accomplished by the joint effort of the iwi and the scientist?

____

____

Text 8: Cook Strait curse

Read the extract below from *Marlborough Midweek* and answer the questions that follow.

Cook Strait curse strikes again

Tom Hunt

Cook Strait travel woes have deepened once more with Bluebridge ferry the *Strait Feronia* parked up with technical issues forcing four sailings to be cancelled.

The ship returned from a routine inspection in Australia and was back in service on Sunday afternoon but a "minor technical glitch" meant it anchored in the Marlborough Sounds rather than coming to Wellington.

Bluebridge Cook Strait ferry Strait Feronia *broke down.*

Ship tracking website **Marinetraffic.com** shows the ferry was anchored north of Picton. A statement from Bluebridge on Monday confirmed the ship had technical problems after its first commercial sailing of Cook Strait on Sunday.

The problem was discovered while the 7.15 pm sailing was still in dock in Picton. The 250 passengers who wanted to transfer were put on another ship, which left at 2.30 am on Monday.

Bluebridge spokesperson Will Dady said four Bluebridge sailings were cancelled on Monday.

"We apologise unreservedly to our passengers for this disruption and are currently rescheduling or refunding those affected."

For Wellington manufacturer Alan Baldwin, it compounded existing problems. His first Picton to Wellington ferry was postponed due to weather last week, then all ferries were cancelled as strong winds lashed the country.

He and his wife caught a flight back from Blenheim but his work ute remained stuck in the South Island.

He had been trying to rebook on the Bluebridge website but said **there was "no hope" of finding a booking for about a month**.

It is the latest in an ongoing saga for Cook Strait ferries, which have been dogged by multiple breakdowns and weather-related cancellations.

Select (✓) the correct answer to the multiple-choice questions below. It is best practice to re-read the text to find the correct answer.

1 What is the main reason that a picture of a ferry is included with this article?

- (A) To advertise bluebridge.co.nz.
- (B) Because it is relevant to the topic of the article.
- (C) To show what a ferry is.
- (D) To provide geographic context.

2 Why had the *Strait Feronia* been in Australia?

- (A) For a routine inspection.
- (B) To fix a broken propeller.
- (C) To add more lifeboats.
- (D) Because of technical problems.

ISBN: 9780170477581

3 How did Bluebridge address the impact of the technical glitch on passengers?

- (A) Bluebridge offered full refunds to passengers.
- (B) Bluebridge quickly repaired the glitch.
- (C) The ferry remained docked in Picton.
- (D) Passengers were transferred to another ship to continue to Wellington.

4 Why does the article reference the website **Marinetraffic.com**?

- (A) Because it looks more professional.
- (B) So that passengers can watch the ferry location live.
- (C) To reinforce that the article is truthful and researched.
- (D) So the Coastguard could find the ferry.

5 After reading the article, you want to find out more about the 'Cook Strait curse' so you google the phrase. Which search result should you click on first?

- (A) https://www.metservice.com/marine/coastal/locations/cook Weather forecast for Cook Strait
- (B) https://en.wikipedia.org/wiki/Cook_Strait Wikipedia page for Cook Strait
- (C) https://nzhistory.govt.nz/media/video/cook-straits-dangerous-waters-roadside-stories Government-owned website about New Zealand History
- (D) https://www.nzherald.co.nz/nz/disruptions-to-cook-strait-ferry-service-due-to-engineering-fault/ 2018 article from the *New Zealand Herald* about the Cook Strait ferry service being delayed

Short-answer questions

We have included short-answer questions here, as they will help you develop your skills in reading texts and understanding the ideas and information that is being presented to you. Practising these skills will help you become faster in finding the answers to the questions when you are in the assessment.

6 What does it mean for passenger Alan Baldwin when he said '***there was "no hope" of finding a booking for about a month***'.

____

____

7 What is the link between the headline '***Cook Strait curse strikes again***' and the content of the article?

____

____

8 Why does the article have quotes from a Bluebridge spokesperson and a passenger?

____

____

9 In your opinion, whose 'woes' are being referred to in this phrase?
'***Cook Strait travel woes have deepened once more***'

____

____

10 Who do you think is the target audience for this article?

____

____

Text 9: Chatham honey tours

Read the extract below from *The New Zealand Beekeeper* and answer the questions that follow.

Chatham honey tours to boost local industry

Chatham Islands beekeeping company Go Wild Apiary is hoping to boost the islands' emerging apiculture industry with a new tourism feature focused on honey.

Go Wild owners Francesca Bonventre and Kaai Silbery are planning Honey Week tours to **coincide** with World Bee Day on May 20 this year. They hope this year's inaugural* event could become an annual celebration of honey that will attract visitors and mainland beekeepers. "We would love for beekeepers to come and see the unique environment we have here for bees and to **meet what we believe to be the last known stock of Black British honey bees**," explains Francesca.

Currently there are around 200 hives on the island, with Go Wild Honey the largest commercial operator. A further dozen families operate the other hives as hobbyists. Francesca explained that Go Wild's success with its **innovative** freeze-dried honey product created the need for more local honey production.

The planned week-long tour would include visits to the islands' apiaries, honey-inspired meals and a special celebration on World Bee Day with an attempt to create the largest ever bee cake. **It would also include local history, a spot of fishing and exploring the birdlife and untamed landscapes of the islands.**

If you are interested in finding out more about the Chatham Islands Honey Week tours, please contact Francesca on: fran@gowild.shop

* inaugural — the first of its kind

Select (✓) the correct answer to the multiple-choice questions below. It is best practice to re-read the text to find the correct answer.

1 *'… planning Honey Week tours to **coincide** with World Bee Day …'*

What is the best word or words to replace 'coincide' in the above sentence?

- (A) correlate
- (B) match
- (C) clash
- (D) happen together

2 *'**meet what we believe to be the last known stock of Black British honey bees**'* means that

- (A) the Black British honey bees are endangered.
- (B) there are too many Black British honey bees.
- (C) you can hold the Black British honey bees.
- (D) you can buy the Black British honey bees.

 ISBN: 9780170477581

3 What does Francesca think led to the need for more honey on the Chatham Islands?

(A) Their tours.
(B) The freeze-dried honey product.
(C) The Black British honey bee.
(D) The World Bee Day celebration.

4 What is the main purpose of this article?

(A) To inform us about Black British honey bees.
(B) To promote the Chatham Islands.
(C) To sell Go Wild honey products.
(D) To inform us about the Honey Week tours.

5 What is the most likely reason that Francesca was quoted in this article?

(A) Because she is a honey bee expert.
(B) Because she is the co-owner of Go Wild.
(C) Because she was born on the Chatham Islands.
(D) Because she works for the magazine.

Short-answer questions

We have included short-answer questions here, as they will help you develop your skills in reading texts and understanding the ideas and information that is being presented to you. Practising these skills will help you become faster in finding the answers to the questions when you are in the assessment.

6 Why has the sentence '***It would also include local history, a spot of fishing and exploring the birdlife and untamed landscapes of the islands.***' been added to the end of the article?

____

____

7 '*… explained that Go Wild's success with its* ***innovative*** *freeze-dried honey product …*'

Why has the word 'innovative' been used in this sentence?

____

____

8 How many hives are there currently on the island?

____

____

9 What is the likely difference between a commercial operator and a hobbyist?

____

____

10 Why has the start and end of the article been put in italics?

____

____

Text 10: Your dog: kibble vs raw feeding

Read the table below from *Canine Weekly* and then the following conversation and answer the questions that follow.

Raw Dog Food vs Kibble: Quick Comparison Already leaning toward one food or the other for your pup? Use this table to quickly decide which diet might be best for your dog.	
If you want …	**Then choose …**
Convenience	Kibble
Better nutrition	Raw
Lower cost	Kibble
Control over ingredients	Raw
Ingredient customization	Either

Jemma: I strongly believe in raw feeding. It's the most natural and biologically appropriate diet for dogs.

Hamish: I do a mix of both kibble and raw food. It gives my dog the benefits of both options.

Matilda: I've always fed my dog kibble, and he's been perfectly healthy.

Harry: I agree with kibble feeding. Raw feeding can actually be dangerous if not done properly.

Jemma: Raw feeding is the best option for dogs. It provides all the necessary nutrients without any fillers or artificial preservatives.

Hamish: But a mix of both provides convenience and variety, while still giving the dog a natural diet.

Matilda: I don't see the need for raw food. Kibble provides everything my dog needs and it's easy to find.

Harry: I agree. Raw food can have harmful bacteria and parasites, and it's hard to make sure it's balanced.

Jemma: If done correctly, raw food is perfectly safe and can provide numerous health benefits for dogs.

Hamish: Exactly. It's important to research and properly prepare raw food to make sure it's balanced and safe for your dog.

Matilda: But kibble is the most convenient and affordable option for many dog owners.

Harry: And it provides all the necessary nutrients for a healthy dog. Raw feeding is just a trend that can be risky.

Select (✓) the correct answer to the multiple-choice questions below. It is best practice to re-read the text to find the correct answer.

1 What is kibble?

- (A) dry dog food
- (B) a breakfast cereal
- (C) a protein snack for dogs
- (D) raw dog food

 ISBN: 9780170477581

2 Looking at the table, why would I choose to feed my dog kibble?

(A) Control over ingredients
(B) Convenience
(C) Better nutrition
(D) Reduce risk of health problems

3 Which person is the most against raw food?

(A) Jemma
(B) Hamish
(C) Matilda
(D) Harry

4 Why does Jemma '*strongly believe in raw feeding*'?

(A) Because kibble is a trend.
(B) It's convenient and affordable.
(C) It's natural and biologically appropriate.
(D) It saves time cooking the meat.

5 Which dog owner advocates for a mixed diet?

(A) Hamish
(B) Jemma
(C) Harry
(D) Matilda

Short-answer questions

We have included short-answer questions here, as they will help you develop your skills in reading texts and understanding the ideas and information that is being presented to you. Practising these skills will help you become faster in finding the answers to the questions when you are in the assessment.

6 Why is it good to read different opinions on dog feeding before making a decision yourself?

___

___

7 What does the conversation suggest about research and informed decision-making?

___

___

8 Identify two reasons for and two reasons against raw feeding in the conversation.

___

___

9 Why do people have such strong opinions about this topic?

___

___

10 How does the conversation suggest that an owner's lifestyle and budget can impact their choice of dog food? Does the table back this up?

___

___

The next step

Now you have looked at 10 different types of text and answered multiple-choice and short-answer questions, the next six texts will have only the multiple-choice questions. This is to replicate more closely the conditions of the Reading assessment, which will mainly offer multiple-choice questions although there may be other types of questions.

Text 11: School embraces RecycleKiwi

Read the extract below from the *CrestClean* website and answer the questions that follow.

School embraces RecycleKiwi as resources rolled out

CrestClean's RecycleKiwi programme has really **struck a chord** with teachers at an Auckland school.

After a RecycleKiwi resource pack was delivered to Red Beach School, a "thank you" card was left for CrestClean business owner Naresh Mani, who takes care of the school's cleaning.

Red Beach teacher Lisa Davies told Naresh the recycling initiative was a **timely** reminder to kids about safeguarding the environment.

"The messages in this resource kit are very **important** for our future generations to understand, so thank you!"

Lisa says the RecycleKiwi resources will be widely used by the youngsters. "Thanks, CrestClean, for the **fabulous** RecycleKiwi kits. We are planning on using them in conjunction with Keep NZ Beautiful Week. All Year 5 and 6 classes will have their own kit."

RecycleKiwi has been developed by CrestClean and the company has delivered free resource packs to more than 500 schools nationwide.

Naresh says he was proud to be involved in the educational programme. "I'm really **excited** by what we are doing.

"CrestClean is doing a great job in promoting recycling to all the schools. It's a brilliant idea."

ISBN: 9780170477581

Select (✓) the correct answer to the multiple-choice questions below. It is best practice to re-read the text to find the correct answer.

1 The resources are being '***rolled out***' means:

- (A) The company is sending materials to schools all at once.
- (B) The company is sending new materials out to some schools.
- (C) The company uses wheels to deliver materials.
- (D) The company is sending rolls of materials to schools.

2 The phrase '***struck a chord***' means:

- (A) The school teaches music.
- (B) The teachers like music.
- (C) The teachers like the RecycleKiwi programme.
- (D) The teachers hit the right notes.

3 Who is in charge of Red Beach School's cleaning?

- (A) Lisa Davies
- (B) RecycleKiwi
- (C) Naresh Mani
- (D) CrestClean

4 Which word from the text best tells you the school really likes this idea?

- (A) timely
- (B) important
- (C) excited
- (D) fabulous

5 In this context, what does sustainable most relate to?

- (A) Saving money.
- (B) Keeping people safe and well.
- (C) Looking after the environment.
- (D) Having a healthy community.

6 The primary purpose of this article is:

- (A) To advertise a product.
- (B) To promote a company.
- (C) To introduce Naresh Mani.
- (D) To fill a newsletter.

Text 12: The Perfect Ring

Read the advertisement below and answer the questions that follow.

ISBN: 9780170477581

Select (✓) the correct answer to the multiple-choice questions below. It is best practice to re-read the text to find the correct answer.

1 What determines the price of the ring?

- (A) using architectural software
- (B) the diamond or gemstone
- (C) handcrafting
- (D) New Zealand gold

2 What ensures the highest quality at an excellent price at Polished Diamonds — Jewellery Design?

- (A) MRI laser scan
- (B) 3D printing
- (C) Virtual CAD modelling
- (D) All of the above.

3 What is the target audience for Polished Diamonds — Jewellery Design based on the information in the text?

- (A) Children and teenagers.
- (B) Adults of all ages.
- (C) Elderly people.
- (D) People interested in diamond rings.

4 Why are images used in the advertisement?

- (A) To distract the viewer.
- (B) To let you know how much it will cost.
- (C) To make you skim past the advert.
- (D) To show an example of what the product could be.

5 Why has the advertisement listed multiple showroom locations?

- (A) To make the text more difficult to understand.
- (B) To inform customers of the showrooms' locations in well-known areas in three cities.
- (C) To limit the target audience of the advertisement.
- (D) To make the product seem less desirable.

Text 13: Kura Māori empowering next generation

Read the extract below from *The Education Gazette Tukutuku Kōrero* and answer the questions that follow.

Kura Māori empowering next generation of engineers in Tairāwhiti

Te Kura Kaupapa Māori O Kawakawa Mai Tawhiti is forging a path for ākonga to pursue careers in STEM, particularly in robotics and engineering.

Breaking cycles and empowering the next generation is the kaupapa for Te Kura Kaupapa Māori O Kawakawa Mai Tawhiti on the far East Coast of Tairāwhiti.

The area school is paving a way forward for promising engineers through its STEM work, currently engaging over 70 ākonga in robotics — and with national success.

A robotics trip to Wellington was an opportunity of many firsts for ākonga, including flying on a plane.

Zoey Henderson leads the kura robotics programme and has witnessed significant strides among students from Years 1 to 13 since the subject was introduced five years ago.

'The children start out in Year 1 and start to develop the skills in terms of coding as they progress,' she explains. 'Once they are in their senior school years, they then start to move into construction and get to test their robots out in an arena setting.'

Last year, a cohort of girls from the te reo Māori immersion kura travelled to Wellington to compete in the VEX Robotics National Championships.

'Our focus last year was to develop our girls' robotics skills as often it is our boys that dominate in this field,' says Zoey.

She says the kura was thankful for sponsorship from the Gattung Foundation — a charitable organisation established in 2022 to help address inequalities for girls and women across Aotearoa.

ISBN: 9780170477581

Select (✓) the correct answer to the multiple-choice questions below. It is best practice to re-read the text to find the correct answer.

1 How long has the school been offering robotics as a subject?

- (A) 10 years
- (B) 5 years
- (C) 2 years
- (D) It has never offered it before.

2 What is the author's purpose in writing this article?

- (A) To show the school's success in producing national champions in robotics.
- (B) To criticise the lack of diversity in the field of robotics and engineering.
- (C) To encourage other schools to start offering robotics as a subject.
- (D) To inform the readers about the positive impact of the school's STEM work in empowering the next generation of engineers in Tairāwhiti.

3 '***Breaking cycles and empowering the next generation***' means:

- (A) Supporting young people to overcome generational barriers and achieve success.
- (B) Encouraging a continuous cycle of poverty and disadvantage.
- (C) Limiting the potential of the younger generation.
- (D) Ignoring the challenges faced by the youth in modern society.

4 How reliable is the information provided in the article?

- (A) The information is entirely made up.
- (B) The information is biased and presents only one side of the story.
- (C) The information is reliable and based on evidence from the school and its students.
- (D) The information is misleading and exaggerates the school's success in robotics.

5 What is the Gattung Foundation and how did it support the kura?

- (A) The Gattung Foundation is a charity that provides scholarships to students interested in arts and culture.
- (B) The Gattung Foundation is a government agency that provides funding to schools for sports activities.
- (C) The Gattung Foundation is a private organisation that promotes the use of technology in education and they donated robots to the kura.
- (D) The Gattung Foundation is a non-profit organisation that supports girls and women in New Zealand and it provided sponsorship to the kura for its robotics programme.

Text 14: A career highlight

Read the adapted article below from the *South Island Lifestyle Magazine* and answer the questions that follow.

A career highlight on the horizon

As I write this article, I'm aware that in a very short time I'll be participating in a lifetime career highlight. I'm excited and just a little nervous, but that's appropriate when you approach significant events.

I'm going to be presenting at a conference. Not unusual for me as I've done this on many occasions over my long tenure, but this time it's different.

It's an international conference for our company's brand and it's taking place in South Africa, where I've learnt they have a strong presence.

I will present on the main stage to a sellout audience on 17th May — and here's my quandary:

What to share with people whose experiences may be totally different at a cultural and business level? How do you create engagement so that their curiosity is piqued and how do you maintain that interest for the duration of the talk so that everyone derives some definite benefit despite my Kiwi accent potentially making hard work of things?

In thinking all of this, I've rationalized that the best place to start is with a process that I've used many times before — and it's stood me in good stead whenever a high level of professionalism is required.

Here's my simple system. Resist procrastinating. It never helps to wait so long that you **find yourself in a corner** ... I prefer to start early.

The next step is always preparation and research. Sure, you've settled on a topic but is what you have to say the latest information?

Then there's timing of everything, hitting your points in the correct order, not relying on notes because they are distracting for you and your audience, and not going off topic.

Lastly, what to wear, given a gal has got to look good, how to open (I'm thinking Te Reo), what resources to provide and how to finish well?

There you have it and soon I'm hoping I'll have done it!!

Wish me luck.

Lynette McFadden
Harcourts Gold Business Owner
0274320474
Lynette_mcfadden@harcourtsgold.co.nz

 ISBN: 9780170477581

Select (✓) the correct answer to the multiple-choice questions below. It is best practice to re-read the text to find the correct answer.

1 What is the author's main purpose in writing this text?

- (A) To inform readers about the process of preparing for a presentation.
- (B) To announce the author's upcoming conference presentation in South Africa.
- (C) To learn te reo Māori.
- (D) To ask for advice on how to navigate cultural and business differences when presenting at an international conference.

2 Which of the following could best replace the phrase '***find yourself in a corner***'?

- (A) find yourself in a circular room
- (B) discover yourself in a painting
- (C) locate yourself in a corner store
- (D) find yourself in a difficult situation

3 What does using personal pronouns in sentences such as '*I'm going to …*', '*I'm excited …*', '*I will present …*' do for the text?

- (A) Makes the text sound more formal and professional.
- (B) Adds a personal touch and helps readers connect with the author's experience.
- (C) Helps to keep the author's identity anonymous.
- (D) Creates confusion for the readers.

4 Why did Lynette McFadden include her phone number and email address at the end of the article?

- (A) To spam readers with marketing messages.
- (B) To make it difficult for readers to contact her.
- (C) To demonstrate her tech-savvy skills.
- (D) To facilitate communication with interested parties who may want to reach out to her.

5 What is the main message a teenager could take out of this article?

- (A) None. The article is irrelevant to teenagers.
- (B) They should focus solely on their appearance and what they wear to events.
- (C) Preparation and research are very important when approaching significant events.
- (D) Procrastinate and wait until the last minute to prepare for important events.

ISBN: 9780170477581

Text 15: Science on the Ice

Read the adapted article below from the *School Journal, November 2018* and answer the questions that follow.

Science on the Ice

Two sets of merino underwear, two fleece jackets, a windbreaker, a puffer jacket, five pairs of gloves, a hat, a balaclava, fleece pants, fleece-lined boots, and lastly — a set of extreme-cold weather gear (called ECWs by those in the know). My kit is issued at Antarctica New Zealand's Christchurch headquarters, and I'm told to return the following morning at six. I'm to wear my ECWs for the flight south. I head for the airport, where I board a plane along with eighty other passengers, most of them scientists. We're ready for temperatures as low as minus 40 degrees Celsius.

The scientists have three main tasks: extracting sediment cores from the sea floor, installing instruments for long-term monitoring, and lowering a tiny, remote-controlled submarine so they can observe the ocean below. 'For me, it's like going to Mars,' says lead oceanographer Craig Stevens. 'We know almost nothing about the ocean beneath the ice shelf — an area that holds the same amount of water as two thousand Lake Taupōs.' Craig is especially interested in ocean currents. 'Oceans absorb heat,' he says, 'and ocean currents **redistribute** this heat. Any change in the climate can affect the force and direction of these currents.'

Craig and his team want to find out if warmer ocean currents are melting the Ross Ice Shelf from beneath. 'Right now, we believe the ice shelf is stable, but it wouldn't take much change in the currents for us to start to see dramatic differences,' he says. The Ross Ice Shelf is significant because it acts like a cork, holding large sections of the West Antarctic Ice Sheet — part of the largest single mass of ice on Earth. In some places, it's up to 2,000 metres thick, and it holds around 90% of the world's freshwater. If the ice sheet were to melt, the world's seas levels would rise by around 5 metres. What would happen after this has been much discussed. For some people, the effects would be catastrophic.

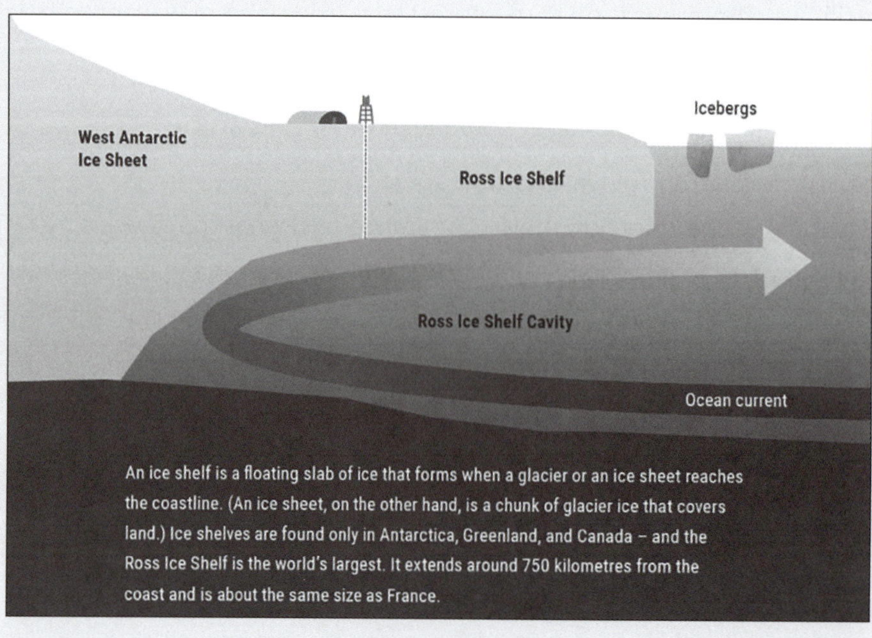

An ice shelf is a floating slab of ice that forms when a glacier or an ice sheet reaches the coastline. (An ice sheet, on the other hand, is a chunk of glacier ice that covers land.) Ice shelves are found only in Antarctica, Greenland, and Canada – and the Ross Ice Shelf is the world's largest. It extends around 750 kilometres from the coast and is about the same size as France.

ISBN: 9780170477581

Select (✓) the correct answer to the multiple-choice questions below. It is best practice to re-read the text to find the correct answer.

1 Why does the author list the items of clothing they were issued to take to Antarctica?

- (A) For fashion purposes.
- (B) Because they couldn't fit it in their luggage.
- (C) To brag about their trip to Antarctica.
- (D) To emphasise how important it is to be prepared for the extremes of Antarctica.

2 Why is Craig Stevens quoted in this article?

- (A) To provide some entertainment to the readers.
- (B) To highlight his lack of knowledge about the ocean beneath the ice shelf.
- (C) To explain the significance of the scientific mission in Antarctica.
- (D) To express his concerns about the safety of the expedition.

3 Why do we trust what Craig Stevens is saying?

- (A) Because he is a skilled athlete.
- (B) Because he is the lead oceanographer for this expedition.
- (C) Because he is a famous celebrity.
- (D) Because he has a degree in a completely unrelated field.

4 What is the best word to replace 'redistribute' in this sentence?

*'… and ocean currents **redistribute** this heat.'*

- (A) transport
- (B) share
- (C) transfer
- (D) disperse

5 What is the purpose of the diagram?

- (A) To help visualise how the warm ocean current is melting the ice pack from underneath.
- (B) To show the underwater scenery near the Ross Ice Shelf.
- (C) To demonstrate the effects of ocean currents on human-made structures in the area.
- (D) To show potential locations for oil drilling in the Ross Sea.

6 If you wanted to find out more about the Ross Ice Shelf, which link would you click on first?

- (A) 'Antarctica's Biggest Mysteries: The Ross Ice Shelf' on the History Channel website: https://www.history.com/news/antarcticas-biggest-mysteries-the-ross-ice-shelf
- (B) 'Top 10 Shocking Facts About the Ross Ice Shelf' on the *Daily Mail* website: https://www.dailymail.co.uk/sciencetech/article-3338868/Top-10-shocking-facts-Ross-Ice-Shelf-Including-signals-hint-underground-lake-beneath-surface.html
- (C) 'The Ross Ice Shelf: a climate change time-bomb?' on the BBC News website: https://www.bbc.com/news/world-46883197
- (D) 'Ross Ice Shelf' on the *National Geographic* website: https://www.nationalgeographic.org/encyclopedia/ross-ice-shelf/

Text 16: Wildboy

Read the article below from *School Journal, May 2016* and answer the questions that follow.

Wildboy: The Journey of Brando Yelavich

You're walking along a wild, lonely stretch of coastline. Suddenly you hear something crashing around in the bush. The mystery creature stumbles onto the beach, and you see it's a goat. What do you do? If you're Brando 'Wildboy' Yelavich, you don't think twice: a goat means dinner. You shoot it, skin it, gut it, and chop it up. Then you bag the pieces and strap the whole lot to your backpack. By the time you set up camp later that night, you'll be grateful for the protein to add to your seaweed stir-fry.

Sound like a day in the life of your average teenager? Amazingly, just a few months earlier, Brando Yelavich had been just that. Living with his sister and parents in suburban Auckland, he had a comfortable existence. There was food in the fridge, so he didn't have to scan the horizon for wild animals when he was hungry, but Brando remembers often feeling depressed and stressed out.

'I fought with my parents about everything,' he says, 'and school was a really bad fit for me. I have ADHD (attention deficit hyperactivity disorder) and dyslexia, and it's taken me a long time to learn that I'm much better in practical situations than in a classroom. After I left school, I went through a few jobs that didn't work out. I ended up lying around doing nothing much. It was a really negative cycle.'

Fascinated by a movie called *Into the Wild* — about the adventures of a young American named Christopher McCandless — Brando began to dream of a completely different life. With a strong urge to achieve something significant, he told his family and friends he was going to become the first person to walk around New Zealand's entire coastline. Hoping to raise $10,000 for Ronald McDonald House, Brando also decided he would be self-sufficient along the way: hunting, fishing, and foraging for food.

Brando walked all those kilometres, and he raised more than $30,000 for his chosen charity. Then he wrote *Wildboy*, a book that went straight onto the bestseller list.

 ISBN: 9780170477581

Select (✓) the correct answer to the multiple-choice questions below. It is best practice to re-read the text to find the correct answer.

1 What is the author's purpose in writing this text?

- (A) To encourage readers to adopt a more adventurous lifestyle and explore the wilderness.
- (B) To inform readers about the benefits of being self-sufficient and relying on natural resources for survival.
- (C) To showcase the success of Brando 'Wildboy' Yelavich and inspire readers to overcome obstacles and pursue their dreams.
- (D) To discuss the ecological impact of hunting and fishing on the New Zealand coastline.

2 What are the main ideas in the text?

- (A) The importance of foraging for food in the wilderness.
- (B) A teenager's journey to self-discovery and accomplishment.
- (C) The dangers of living in the wilderness alone.
- (D) The history and culture of New Zealand's coastline.

3 Why has the author used a rhetorical question in this line?

*'**Sound like a day in the life of your average teenager?**'*

- (A) To engage the reader and make them reflect on the scenario presented.
- (B) To test the reader's knowledge about the habits of teenagers.
- (C) To get the reader to provide an answer out loud.
- (D) To convey a message of dismay in teenagers.

4 What is the best word to replace 'Fascinated' in this sentence?

'***Fascinated** by a movie called* Into the Wild …'

- (A) Captivated
- (B) Confused
- (C) Amused
- (D) Scared

5 What clues are there that the target audience for this text is teenagers?

- (A) Use of informal language.
- (B) References to teenage topics such as school and family conflict.
- (C) Focus on a young person's journey of self-discovery.
- (D) All of the above.

6 What was the difference between how much money Brando hoped to raise for Ronald McDonald House and how much he did raise?

- (A) Approximately $500.
- (B) Approximately $5000.
- (C) Approximately $10,000.
- (D) Approximately $20,000.

Let's be accurate

Kia tika tātou

The Literacy Writing assessment (US 32405) will expect you to be accurate in your writing. You will write two pieces on two different topics. Then you will be given a separate question with tasks that will check your knowledge of correct English language use.

These questions may be about:

- essential punctuation: capital letters and full stops
- other punctuation marks: comma, exclamation mark, question mark, speech marks
- use of the apostrophe for possession
- use of the apostrophe for contracted verbs
- sentences: short (or simple) and long (or compound, complex) with conjunctions
- tenses
- spelling.

You know something about all of these things. Here, we are going to remind you of the **basic skills** you need for this assessment.

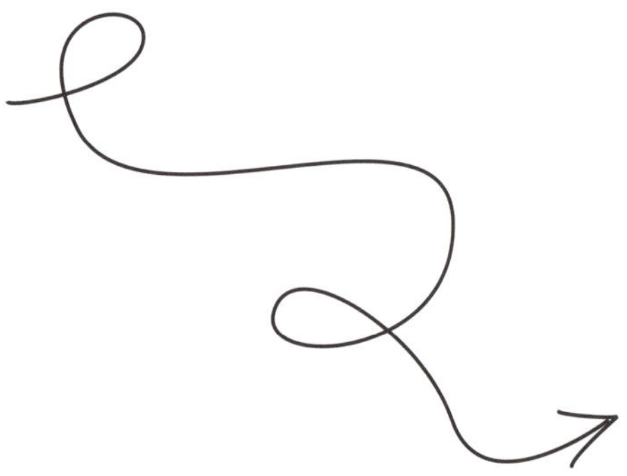

 ISBN: 9780170477581

Punctuation — the basics

The capital letter

1 Sentences always start with a capital letter.

For example: **M**y best friend lives next door.

2 A proper noun is the specific name of a person, place or thing and it needs a capital letter.

For example: **M**y best friend, **M**oana, lives next door.

3 The main words in titles of books, films, plays, songs, etc. are written in capital letters.

For example: **M**y best friend, **M**oana, who lives next door, loves the movie ***M****oana*.

4 Capital letters begin the first word inside speech marks.

For example: **M**y best friend, **M**oana, said, '**L**et's go and see ***M****oana* at the movies.'

'I' or 'i'?
'I' is the personal pronoun. It is **always** a capital letter.
- **I** asked Dad if **I** could go to the pool and he said that **I** could.

YOUR TURN

Overwrite the words in each sentence that need a capital letter.

1 in april, my family is going to brisbane to see our cousin wiremu.
(You will need 4 of them.)

2 jack and jill went up to auckland to see *battle of the teen bands*.
(You will need 6 of them.)

3 my sister eats an apple every day, but i hate apples.
(You will need 2 of them.)

4 i hope i get a Bike for my birthday because my old one is useless.
(You will need to add 2 and remove 1 of them.)

5 we're flying to samoa for christmas to stay with family in apia.
(You will need 4 of them.)

ISBN: 9780170477581

The full stop (.)

Sentences always end with a full stop.

For example: The lemon tree produces juicy lemons all year long.

YOUR TURN

Without changing the order of the words, add the missing capital letters and full stops.

1 there is a park at the end of my street i go there most weekends if my friend Aroha is around she comes too *(Make 3 sentences.)*

2 my duvet is on the floor my books are on the floor my clothes are on the floor I get called untidy I don't know why *(Make 5 sentences.)*

3 Ōtaki is an area with lots of attractions for visitors Ōtaki has so much to see and do it's a hidden gem in the greater Wellington region *(Make 3 sentences.)*

4 mars is a cold desert world it is half the size of Earth mars is sometimes called the Red Planet it's red because of rusty iron in the ground *(Make 4 sentences.)*

5 to make Rocky Road bring a pot of water to the boil with a glass bowl on top gently melt the chocolate in the bowl, stirring constantly remove once fully melted *(Make 3 sentences.)*

The question mark (?)

A question mark is placed at the end of a sentence that asks a direct question.

For example:

- Are you cold**?**
- Can I help you**?**
- 'Will you stop chewing so loudly**?**' asked Dad**.**

However, the sentences below are not direct questions. They do not need a question mark.

- My mother always asks me if I'm cold.
- My boss tells me to ask customers if I can help them.
- My dad asked me to stop chewing so loudly.

Because the question mark behaves just like a full stop and forms the end of the sentence, you do not need a full stop as well. Look carefully and you will see the question mark includes a full stop: **?** Remember: the next sentence must start with a capital letter.

YOUR TURN

Put a question mark into any of these sentences that need one.

1 May we go to the park, Mum.

2 Everyone asks me if I'm going in the talent competition.

3 You don't like coffee, do you.

4 If it's raining, how come the sun is shining.

5 'Can you send me the link' asked Joe.

It's different in other languages.
In Spanish, for example,
*¿Qué hora es***?**
means
*What time is it***?**

 ISBN: 9780170477581

The exclamation mark (!)

The exclamation mark is placed at the end of an order, an exclamation with strong emotion, or when somebody is shouting.

For example:

- Ouch**!**
- Eat your dinner**!**
- Stop**!**
- Pass the ball**!**
- Get out**!**
- What a terrible thing to say**!**

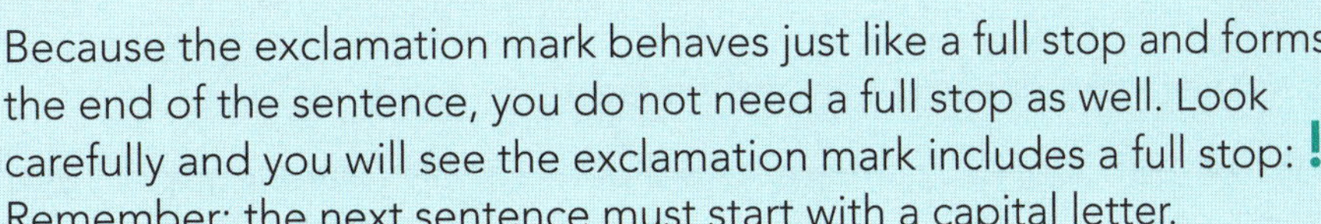

Because the exclamation mark behaves just like a full stop and forms the end of the sentence, you do not need a full stop as well. Look carefully and you will see the exclamation mark includes a full stop: **!** Remember: the next sentence must start with a capital letter.

YOUR TURN

These sentences need exclamation and/or question marks. Put them in.

1 I am so scared. Will it hurt.

2 We'll be late, hurry up. You're so slow.

3 Is it much further.

4 That test was so easy. I wonder if I'll pass with flying colours.

5 Hey, budding astronomers, listen up. How well do you know your own solar system. Can you put the planets in the proper order. This interactive game helps students to sort out the planets and it's fun.

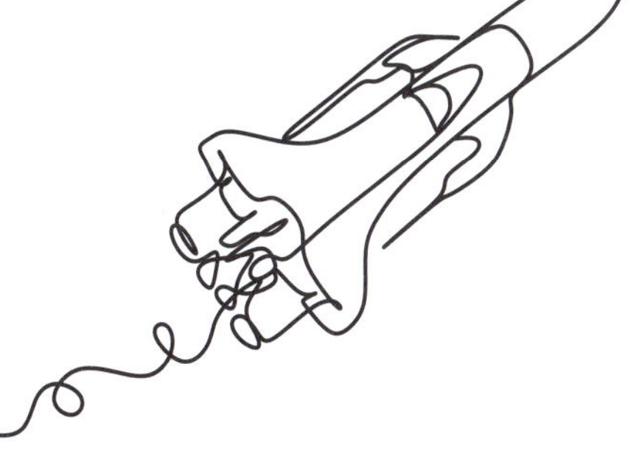

The comma (,)

A comma is used to show a pause in a sentence.

For example: When she goes to the netball court, Sunita practises shooting first and then dribbling.

A comma separates items in a list.

For example: The most common sciences include Biology, Mathematics, Physics, Chemistry and Social Science.

Test to see if you need a comma. Read the sentence out loud and if you take a small breath, then that's where you put a comma.

YOUR TURN

Add commas to these sentences to make them easier to read.

1 Sunita went to the shop to buy streamers balloons candles party poppers and a cake for the birthday party.

2 My brother who is the hungriest person in the world just loves hamburgers.

3 Every week at half past six on a Sunday morning I get up put on my running shoes and go for a ten-kilometre run.

4 'I'm going to feed the chooks' said Janet.

See if you can find good places for at least 4 commas in this piece from a website about eating more vegetables.

5 Chop up vegetables (peppers carrots celery) and toss them into your favourite chilli recipe. If you don't like vegetables much sneak them into foods you do enjoy (like grating carrots into tomato sauce or again courgettes into bread). It's a great way to get your veggies without having to taste them!

Speech marks (' … ' or " … ")

Speech marks are also called **inverted commas** or **quotation marks**.

A Speech marks are used to show direct speech — the words spoken.

For example: 'Kia ora,' called Mele from across the street.

Remember, every new speaker's words start on a new line. For example:

'Kia ora,' called Mele.
'Hi, where are you off to?' replied James.
'Nowhere,' muttered Mele.

 ISBN: 9780170477581

B Inverted commas can show the title of a movie, or play or book, etc.

For example: **'**Avatar**'** is my favourite movie.

However, this can also be shown by using italics if you are typing.

For example: *Avatar* is my favourite movie.

C Speech marks can show words quoted from what someone has said or words someone has written.

For example: The words **'**Take care of our children. Take care of what they hear: take care of what they feel. For how the children grow, will be the shape of Aotearoa**'** are a quote from Dame Whina Cooper.

YOUR TURN

1 Add speech marks to this short passage.

It's six o'clock and here's the latest news, burbled the radio.

Sitiveni, where are you? yelled Mum.

Here, he whispered. Shh, don't bark, he said to the dog.

A tornado has struck up north … the radio droned on.

2 Add inverted commas to this passage.

When I was younger, my favourite book was The Twits by Roald Dahl. I particularly liked the chapter called The Great Upside Down Monkey Circus.

3 Add inverted commas to this sentence.

I solemnly swear that I am up to no good is said by Harry Potter when he wants to use the Marauder's Map.

Apostrophe (')

A **The apostrophe is used to show a contraction** — where one or more letters are missed out, contracting two words into one.

For example:
I **do not** want to go. I **don't** want to go.
He will never be able to climb that fence. **He'll** never be able to climb that fence.

I **should have** got up earlier. (Not 'I should of'.)
I **should've** got up earlier.

They **would have** arrived on time if the bus **had not** broken down. (Not 'They would of'.)
They **would've** arrived on time if the bus **hadn't** broken down.

ISBN: 9780170477581

B The apostrophe is used to show possession with an s ('s).

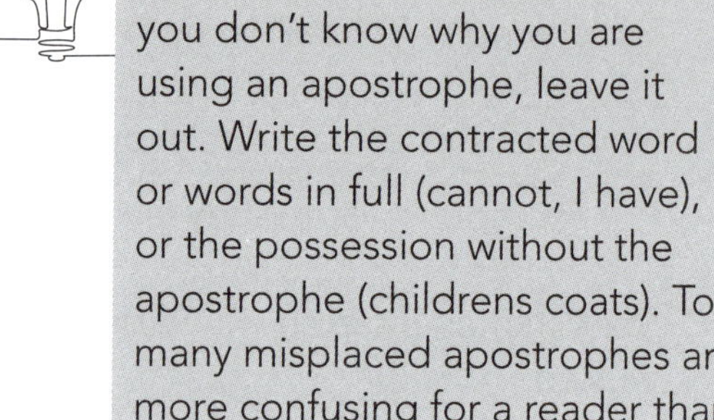

TIP: If in doubt, leave it out. If you don't know why you are using an apostrophe, leave it out. Write the contracted word or words in full (cannot, I have), or the possession without the apostrophe (childrens coats). Too many misplaced apostrophes are more confusing for a reader than the occasional missing one.

For example:

- the recipe's instructions
- a circle's radius
- the magician's best card trick

We can get confused when the 'owner' is a word ending in 's'. Write the word first (bus), then add 's for ownership.

For example:

- This bus's seats are red.
- The two friends' shoes got mixed up at the wharenui.

NOTE: the last 's' is sometimes left off if the word is easier to pronounce without it.

YOUR TURN

Each sentence needs two apostrophes. Add them.

1 Six childrens coats were left on the school bus, but the driver didnt want to look after them.

2 Huans favourite subject is Geography because hes a whizz at drawing maps.

3 It shouldve rained today, but instead the suns heat was intense.

4 Its easy to talk about getting fit, but its not easy to do it!

5 Ariki cant find his footy kit because Ive hidden it in the shed.

You probably know there's a lot more to learn about punctuation, but for now these are the basics. If you can understand when and how to use these, you are well on your way to achieving the Literacy Writing assessment.

ISBN: 9780170477581

Sentences — the basics

We are going to look at the essentials of sentence structure. There is a lot more to learn about sentences, but what is important for this assessment is that you know the basics well.

What is a simple sentence?

A simple sentence is a group of words put together to make one thought, one idea. Each sentence begins with a capital letter and ends with a full stop. **Always.**

- **Elisapeta ate.**
- **Elisapeta ate** breakfast.
- **Elisapeta ate** breakfast in the kitchen.
- **Elisapeta ate** breakfast in the kitchen early this morning.
- **Elisapeta ate** eggs for breakfast in the kitchen early this morning.

Each one of the lines is a single sentence. Each one contains one idea about Elisapeta.

Sentences can be long and still have just the one idea.

You know this.
Just remember to start with a CAPITAL LETTER and end with a full stop (.) for every sentence you write.

What is a compound sentence?

A compound sentence is a sentence with two ideas.

Sentences can have more than one idea. Remember your chemistry. *A compound: a thing composed of two or more separate elements.*

- Elisapeta ate breakfast but she didn't brush her teeth.

This sentence has two ideas and could be two separate sentences, but they are joined together with the word **but**.

Idea 1: Elisapeta ate her breakfast.

Idea 2: She didn't brush her teeth.

Elisapeta ate breakfast **but** she didn't brush her teeth.

Idea 1 — joining word conjunction — Idea 2

What is a conjunction?

A conjunction is a connecting word. It glues words, phrases or parts of a sentence together.

The day was sunny **and** windy.

Joining two words.

Essentially it joins two or more sentences into a single sentence. For example:

It was perfect for sailing **so** we headed for the marina.

Joining two sentences to make one sentence.

Conjunctions are usually found in the middle of sentences, but some may be used to begin a sentence.

For example: The boat sailed beautifully well **although** it was small.

could be written as:

Although the boat was small, it sailed beautifully well.

Here are the most common conjunctions:

after	also	although	and
as	because	before	but
for	however	if	nevertheless
nor	or	since	so
still	than	then	though
unless	until	when	where
whether	which	while	yet

The main conjunctions are **for**, **and**, **nor**, **but**, **or**, **yet**, **so**. Some students learn the acronym 'FANBOYS' to remember this.

Choosing the correct conjunction depends on what you want to say. Look at these examples:

Jodie likes toast **and** cereal for breakfast.

Jodie likes toast **but** prefers cereal for breakfast.

Jodie likes toast **or** cereal for breakfast.

Each sentence says something different because of the conjunction that has been chosen.

ISBN: 9780170477581

YOUR TURN

Join each set of sentences into one sentence by using appropriate conjunctions.
You do not need to change the order of the words.
You might use these conjunctions: *and, because, but, however, so, while, yet, although.*

Write your answers on the lines below. Remember to change the capital letters.

1 Sione waited for the train. It was running late. He knew he'd miss soccer practice.

2 We needed a place to study. We went to the library. It was quiet there.

3 I asked for a lemon ice block. The shopkeeper gave me an orange one.

4 Aroha whispered her question. We were in class. She got me in trouble.

5 I'm wearing a woolly jersey. I'm still cold.

What is a run-on sentence?

A run-on sentence is a sentence that contains more than one idea without proper punctuation.

One problem that many students have with their writing is the run-on sentence — essentially, they don't know when to *stop*.

Here's one way of looking at this problem:

You know that two simple complete sentences can be joined with a conjunction, like this.

It was a sunny day, **so** I put on lots of sun block.

If you omit the conjunction **so** and put nothing else in its place (like a semicolon), then the sentence is a run-on sentence, like this:

It was a sunny day I put on lots of sun block.

Essentially, that is two sentences that have fused together. Check that your sentences have the conjunctions they need.

Remember, a paragraph does not consist of one single sentence. Use punctuation!

and ... and ... and ...

We use the word **and** a lot to join sentences together. Sometimes too often.

Read these sentences aloud. Can you hear how the second example sounds less breathless and segmented, more smooth and joined together?

1 Tom went to the swimming pool every day **and** he swam for an hour before school **and** an hour after school **and** he got really fit **and** he went in the trials for the school team **and** he got in.

2 Tom went to the swimming pool every day **where** he swam for an hour before school **and** an hour after school. **He** got really fit **so** he went in the trials for the school team **and** he got in.

We're not saying don't use **and** ... just don't overuse it.

YOUR TURN

Rewrite each of these run-on sentences into four sentences. You may add or remove conjunctions if you need to do so.

1 Whakapapa is a brilliant place to go for skiing and snowboarding and you can stay nearby at National Park, but we stay at Ohakune because my aunt has a place there that we can use and we drive over to Whakapapa every day to ski.

2 I love to play basketball I'm allowed to play each night for an hour outside the garage at home I would play all day, every day if I could my sister shoots hoops with me.

3 Orienteering is a great way to keep fit and to learn navigation skills anyone can join a club we start on white courses they are the easiest then the yellow orange and red ones get harder clubs help people to learn.

ISBN: 9780170477581

Tenses — the basics

In English, *when* something happens is shown by the verb form. Here, we will just deal with the three main verb forms, **past**, **present** and **future**. You might think of this as **yesterday**, **today** and **tomorrow**.

Past	Present	Future
I walked to school.	I walk to school.	I will walk to school.
He worked after school.	He works after school.	He will work after school.
They danced in class.	They dance in class.	They will dance in class.

Notice how the future tense adds the word *will* in front of the verb.

Unfortunately, it's not this easy with the past tense. There are many irregular verbs that do not use the **-ed** form for past tense.

- I said — not 'sayed'
- I ate — not 'eated'
- I thought — not 'thinked'
- I blew — not 'blowed'
- I broke — not 'breaked'
- I brought — not 'bringed'

- He sat — not 'sitted'
- He went — not 'goed'
- He found — not 'finded'
- He bought — not 'buyed'
- He got — not 'getted'
- He saw — not 'seed'

If you have a younger sibling, you might have heard them putting the -ed ending on words and having to learn the 'correct' way to make a past tense.

YOUR TURN

Change the tense from future to past. Change 'tomorrow' to 'yesterday'.

1 I will eat my dinner at a café tomorrow.

____

2 Huan will drive to school in his mum's car tomorrow.

____

3 Mieke will choose a new dress tomorrow.

____

4 They will know their results tomorrow.

____

Here's a young child's story. Correct all the incorrect past-tense verbs.

5 I sayed to my teddy that we goed to the mall yesterday. We bringed back some new paints. Then I drawed a picture of him when he falled off the shelf. After that, we eated dinner and he sleeped in my bed.

Students sometimes get past, present and future mixed up. However, you will probably be able to hear what sounds correct if you read a sentence out loud.

ISBN: 9780170477581

Spelling — the basics

English spelling can be really difficult. However, there are patterns for most words. Here's one example:

The word **station** is often spelled **stashun** by young children learning to write because the ending sounds like **shun**.

Once you learn that it is spelled **station**, you see that lots of other words fall into this pattern, words like:

action	caption	education	junction	fraction
nation	option	potion	motion	ration

Look for patterns.

Homophones

English does have a lot of words that sound the same but are spelled differently for different meanings. These are called homophones.

I **knew** I wanted a **new** coat.
A **whole** doughnut may have a **hole** in the middle.
I picked up a **pair** of shoes under the **pear** tree.
He wrote a **piece** about **peace** for the magazine.
Can you **hear** me? I'm right **here**.
I am unsure **whether** the **weather** will be sunny or rainy tomorrow.

YOUR TURN

1 In this sentence, would you use **sight** or **site**?

My dad works on a building ________________.

2 How about this one — **write** or **right**?

I'm going to ________________ a letter to my cousin.

A good way to practise using the correct version is to write one sentence using both words to show you know the meaning of each one. Choose the right word from the brackets to complete each sentence.

3 The ____________ brought in a tray of fine cakes the cook had ____________. (*maid, made*)

4 I ____________ my shirt looked ____________, but it was really old. (*new, knew*)

5 I dropped through the ____________ in the ground and below me was a ____________ new world. (*hole, whole*)

6 Whenever ____________ a fine day, the cat stalks around ____________ territory. (*its, it's*)

The only way to get this correct is to know the meaning and spelling of both words. One of the very best ways to learn the meaning and spelling of words is to read a lot.

ISBN: 9780170477581

Practise your reading in the reading section of this book. It will help your spelling in the writing section!

English spelling can be tricky. Try explaining these to a person your age learning English:

- four, forty, fourth
- nine, ninety, ninth.

Impossible, right? Just learn the words!

You need to learn the words you spell incorrectly often. If spellcheck keeps correcting the same words for you, take some time to learn the correct version for yourself. The good old spelling test with a friend will help.

There are some words that students often find tricky. Spend some time checking that you can spell them correctly.

- definitely
- responsible
- separate
- embarrass
- occurrence
- unnecessary
- acceptable
- particularly
- especially
- liquefy
- conscience
- parallel
- friend
- a lot (you never write 'alittle', so don't write 'alot')

If you need more help with written English, try:

Now you are ready to practise answering the type of questions you will get in the third question of the Writing assessment. This question focuses on exercises relating to language use.

Here are some language tasks that are similar to those you will meet in the assessment ...

Practice set 1

1 Which words finish the sentence accurately?

At my house __ ___ not allowed to have a phone in the bedroom.

(A) i am
(B) I am
(C) I'm not
(D) I cannot

2 Select the correct punctuation for direct speech.

We're heading out now called Mum.

(A) 'We're heading out now, called Mum.
(B) 'We're heading out now' called Mum.
(C) We're heading out now,' called Mum.
(D) 'We're heading out now,' called Mum.

3 Which full stop and capital letter creates two accurate sentences?

I'm having dinner at Gran's tonight she's cooking spag bol.

(A) tonight. She's
(B) dinner. At
(C) cooking. Spag bol.

4 Possession: select the correct word to complete the sentence accurately.

Six ___________ coats were left at school yesterday.

(A) childrens
(B) children's
(C) childrens'
(D) child'rens

5 Select the best comma placement.

Mikaere packed a sleeping bag two pairs of socks and a torch.

(A) packed, a
(B) bag, two
(C) and, a
(D) socks, and

6 Apostrophe: select the correct word to complete the sentence accurately.

___ a long walk home if you miss the bus.

(A) Its
(B) Its'
(C) it's
(D) It's

7 What punctuation is needed to finish the sentence accurately?

'Are you going to work now

(A) .'
(B) ,
(C) ?'
(D) ?

8 Put the following sentences in the best order.

(A) At our school the students are asked to keep everywhere clean.
(B) They are usually good at putting their own litter in the bin.
(C) Everyone is responsible for looking after the environment.
(D) They also enjoy playing in a clean playground.

Best order:

 ISBN: 9780170477581

Practice set 2

1 Select the correct word to finish the sentence accurately.

_______ ask me again, I won't go!

- (A) Dont
- (B) Doesn't
- (C) Dont'
- (D) Don't

2 Select the correct verb to complete the sentence accurately.

I _________ a plate of biscuits to the party last night.

- (A) brought
- (B) bought
- (C) bringed
- (D) bring

3 Select the correct form of the verb to complete the sentence accurately.

Our team never ______ a game.

- (A) looses
- (B) loses
- (C) losers
- (D) lose

4 Select the correctly written pronoun to complete the sentence accurately.

My tortoise sleeps in ______ shell all day long.

- (A) Its
- (B) its
- (C) it's
- (D) its'

5 Select the correctly spelled word to complete the sentence accurately.

Mei is ______ going on holiday tomorrow.

- (A) definitely
- (B) definately
- (C) definitley
- (D) definitly

6 Which sentence is punctuated correctly?

- (A) Matiu asked "what's for dinner?"
- (B) Matiu asked, "What's for dinner?"
- (C) Matiu asked, "What's for dinner."
- (D) Matiu asked "What's for dinner?"

7 Put the following sentences in the best order.

- (A) I like the slide the best.
- (B) Everyone goes there a lot.
- (C) It's got lots of climbing frames, too.
- (D) Our local park is a great place for kids.

Best order:

8 Which punctuation mark finishes the second sentence correctly?

The mean of 5, 19 and a third number is 15. Calculate the third number

- (A) .
- (B) ?
- (C) !
- (D) ,

Practice set 3

1 Which sentence is punctuated correctly?

- (A) 'My whānau will celebrate Matariki with a hāngi,' said Tama. 'Can I come?' asked Mele.
- (B) My whānau will celebrate Matariki with a hāngi, said Tama. 'Can I come?' asked Mele.
- (C) 'My whānau will celebrate Matariki with a hāngi,' said Tama. Can I come? asked Mele.
- (D) 'My whānau will celebrate Matariki with a hāngi,' said Tama. 'Can I come?' asked Mele.

2 Select the line with accurate use of the comma in this sentence.

You can use a number of functions on your calculator to add subtract multiply and divide fractions.

- (A) … add, subtract
- (B) … add, subtract, multiply
- (C) … add, subtract, multiply, and divide

3 Select the correctly punctuated word to complete the sentence accurately.

Miriam _____ hungry.

- (A) wasnt'
- (B) wasnt
- (C) wasn't
- (D) was'nt

4 Select the correctly spelled word to complete the sentence accurately.

Choir practice is ____________ after school today.

- (A) imediately
- (B) immediatley
- (C) immediately
- (D) immedietly

5 Select the correct word to complete the sentence accurately.

Bai _________ gone to soccer practice but he lost his boots.

- (A) would've
- (B) would of
- (C) wood of
- (D) wouldv'e

6 Which words in these two sentences need capital letters?

In 1958 a submarine called the uss nautilus sailed beneath the frozen ice of the arctic ocean. This was proof that the enormous ice sheet rests on water and not land.

- (A) USS, Arctic
- (B) Nautilus, Arctic Ocean
- (C) USS, Ice Sheet
- (D) USS, Nautilus, Arctic Ocean

7 Select the correct verb to complete the sentence accurately.

Otis ____ at home tomorrow because he's ill.

- (A) stays
- (B) will stay
- (C) stayed
- (D) staid

8 Select the correct word to complete the sentence accurately.

Tane has _______ of friends and they all play touch together.

- (A) a lot
- (B) alot
- (C) allot
- (D) a lott

ISBN: 9780170477581

Practice set 4

1 Select the correct word to complete the sentence.

In July _____ midwinter here.

(A) it's
(B) its
(C) its'

2 Select the correct form of the verb to complete the sentence accurately.

Jill ________ to the park after her ballet class yesterday.

(A) goes
(B) will go
(C) went
(D) is going

3 Which line is correctly punctuated?

(A) 'Oh help!' 'Oh no!' It's a Gruffalo.
(B) 'Oh help! Oh no! It's a Gruffalo.'
(C) 'Oh help! Oh no!' 'It's a Gruffalo.'
(D) 'Oh help! Oh no!' It's a Gruffalo.'

4 Select the best place to put a comma into this sentence.

When asked to round up to two decimal places this means there should be exactly two digits after the decimal point.

(A) up, to
(B) places, this
(C) means, there

5 Select the correct word to complete the sentence accurately.

Siva ________ gone to netball practice yesterday.

(A) should of
(B) should
(C) should've
(D) shouldv'e

6 Which sentence is correct?

(A) the all blacks are playing in Auckland next week.
(B) The All blacks are playing in auckland next week.
(C) The All Blacks are playing in auckland next week.
(D) The All Blacks are playing in Auckland next week.

7 Select all the words that need a capital letter in this sentence.

The wheel blacks team is made up of a core of paralympians that represented new zealand at the tokyo 2020 paralympic games.

(A) Wheel, Blacks, New, Zealand, Paralympic
(B) Paralympians, New, Zealand, Tokyo, Paralympic
(C) Wheel, Blacks, Paralympians, New, Zealand, Tokyo, Paralympic, Games
(D) Wheel, Blacks, Team, New, Zealand, Tokyo, Paralympic, Games

8 Select the correct spelling to complete the sentence accurately.

'Bluff oysters are wild ______ and their creamy-coloured meat is delicate and succulent.' The Seafood Collective.

(A) cort
(B) caught
(C) catched
(D) court

Practice set 5

1 Select the sentence with correct use of capital letters.

- (A) Sitiveni and i went to new Plymouth.
- (B) sitiveni and I went to New Plymouth.
- (C) Sitiveni and I went to New Plymouth.
- (D) Sitiveni and I went to new Plymouth.

2 Select the correct word to complete the sentence accurately.

Talia and her sister Arihi are spending Christmas in Samoa at _____ grandmother's village.

- (A) they're
- (B) there
- (C) their

3 Select the best place to add a full stop to make two complete sentences.

Tilda is going camping next week she wants to get an idea of how heavy her pack will be without actually packing it.

- (A) camping. Next
- (B) be, Without
- (C) week. She

4 Select the correctly spelled word to complete the sentence.

Rohan ____________ a birthday gift from his uncle in Delhi.

- (A) recieved
- (B) received
- (C) resieved
- (D) receeved

5 What punctuation is needed to finish the sentence?

Mere shouted, 'I'm never playing hockey again

- (A) .
- (B) !
- (C) !'
- (D) '

6 Put the following sentences in the best order.

- (A) I don't think a couple of hours is too much if I'm doing work.
- (B) For example, yesterday I got told off when I was looking up information on the internet for a school project.
- (C) My mother is always telling me to put down my phone.
- (D) Personally, I don't think I use my phone too much at all.

Best order:

7 Select the correct form of the verb to complete the sentence accurately.

If I ________ this glass it will smash.

- (A) drop
- (B) dropped
- (C) will drop
- (D) have dropped

8 Select the best place to put a comma in this sentence.

Sophie took a deep breath picked up her violin and started to play.

- (A) Sophie, took
- (B) breath, picked
- (C) violin, and
- (D) and, started

ISBN: 9780170477581

Practice set 6

1 Select the correct word to complete the sentence accurately.

From 160-storey buildings to bridges that span 165 km, _________ engineering minds and high-end technology have come together to create the impossible.

- (A) todays
- (B) todays'
- (C) today's
- (D) to'days

2 Select the correct form of the verb to complete the sentence accurately.

Learn about how daily phenomenon and nature _____ _______ an inspiration in many of these creations.

- (A) were being
- (B) have been
- (C) has been
- (D) was being

3 Select the punctuation mark that completes the sentence.

We seem preoccupied with the soil and rocks of Mars … ever wonder what the world beneath the surface looks like

- (A) .
- (B) ?"
- (C) !
- (D) ?

4 Select the correct pronoun to complete the sentence accurately.

The purpose of this mission is what ____ always been – to learn.

- (A) its
- (B) it's
- (C) It's
- (D) its'

5 Select the best comma placement for this sentence.

Imagine building a robot a helicopter a camera packaging it up and sending it on rockets to a tiny dot in the sky. To Mars!

- (A) a robot, a helicopter, a camera
- (B) a camera, packaging
- (C) a robot, a helicopter, a camera packaging it up, and
- (D) a robot, a helicopter, a camera, packaging

6 Which words in this sentence need capital letters?

perseverance launched on the atlas V-541 rocket on 30 july 2020 and will reach mars on 18 february 2021, landing in an area called the jezero crater.

- (A) Perseverance, Mars, February, Jezero
- (B) Atlas, July, February, Jezero
- (C) Perseverance, Atlas, July, Mars, February, Jezero, Crater
- (D) Perseverance, July, Mars, February, Jezero, Crater

7 Select the correct adjective to complete the sentence accurately.

For this month's article, I want to talk about one of the _______ bridges in the world: the Charilaos Trikoupis Bridge.

- (A) most fine
- (B) fine
- (C) finiest
- (D) finest

8 Select the correct spelling of the travel time taken before the bridge was built to complete the sentence accurately.

This bridge has significantly reduced travel time between the two towns from over ______ minutes to a mere seven minutes.

- (A) forty
- (B) fourty
- (C) forteen
- (D) fortie

Practice set 7

1 Select the correct version of this incorrect sentence.

me and my best friend are going to the latest Fast & Furious movie.

A My best freind and I are going to see the latest Fast & Furious movie.
B My best friend and i are going to see the latest Fast & Furious movie.
C Me and my best freind are going to see the latest Fast & Furious movie.
D My best friend and I are going to see the latest Fast & Furious movie.

2 Select the correct pronoun to complete the sentence accurately.

'It's time you took _____dog for a walk,' said Mum.

A you're
B your
C youre
D yore

3 Select the correct words to complete the sentence accurately.

________ a new family next door. ___________ got a massive dog.

A Theirs they've
B Theres theyve
C There's They've
D there's They've

4 Select the correct word to complete the question accurately.

____ socks are these left in the changing room?

A Who's
B Whose
C Whos
D Who'se

5 Select the correct words to complete the sentence accurately.

If it's _____ o'clock already then I'm _____ late to get _____ rehearsal on time.

A to too, two
B two, too, to
C to, two, too
D two, to, too

6 Select the correct pronoun to complete the sentence accurately.

Please tell me, which house is _______?

A theirs
B their's
C theirs'
D their

7 Select the correctly spelled word to complete the sentence accurately.

It is ___________ difficult to spell some words!

A expecially
B espeshally
C especially
D especialy

8 Choose the correct form of the verb to complete this sentence accurately.

Marama takes the bus to town where she ______ into every shop window in the main street.

A looked
B is looking
C will look
D looks

ISBN: 9780170477581

Let's get writing

Kia tuhi tātou

As part of the Literacy Writing assessment (US 32405), you will be expected to:

- write two pieces of different text types
- write in formal English.

Both text types will be specified (letter, email, article, an online piece, etc.) and you will write on topics which are related to everyday life. Topics may be things like school issues, sport, community, environment, staying healthy, important individuals and finding employment.

In general, the writing you do will be formal. You are being asked to demonstrate that you are able to choose formal words, structures and techniques that are appropriate to the piece you are asked to write.

There will also be some questions on written language techniques such as spelling, sentences and punctuation. We have given you examples of these questions in the **Let's be accurate** section of this book.

Elements of successful writing

Before you can be successful in the assessment, you need to make sure that you have the best approach to writing. Let's take a look at the four key elements you need to be aware of.

Audience and purpose	**Planning**
• Who your audience is and how to write appropriately for that audience • What the purpose of the piece is and how to write appropriately for that purpose	• Brainstorming for ideas • Deciding on your ideas and examples • Organising ideas and examples into groupings
Structure • Effective organisation of ideas into paragraphs • Giving each paragraph a purpose • Creating clear paragraph progression • Meeting the word limit	**Checking your writing** • Correct spelling • Correct use of punctuation • Effective word choice • Accurate sentence structure

Let's take a closer look at each of these boxes.

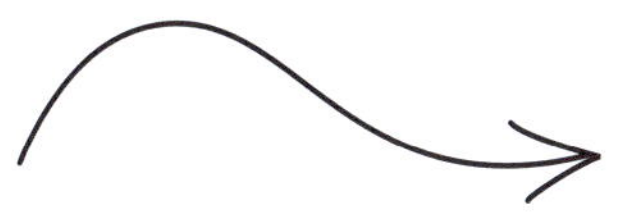

ISBN: 9780170477581

Audience and purpose

The first important things to take note of are:

1 **Who** will be reading what you write (**audience**).

2 **What** you are trying to achieve with your writing (**purpose**).

The assessment question will tell you your audience and purpose. Make sure you keep both in mind as you write. Here are some examples:

Audience You may be writing for: • your fellow students in a class magazine • your principal in a formal letter • your school community in a school newsletter • people your age in an online forum • your local community in a newspaper • a local business owner • your grandparent or other relative and so on.	**Purpose** Your purpose may be to: • **persuade** others to join you in a venture • **explain** the reasons why you believe something is true • **thank** someone for a gift or favour • **offer** help to an organisation • **inform** people about an issue you think is important • make a polite **complaint** and so on.

A closer look at audience and purpose

Let's take a look at a possible assessment question.

Your school is running an International Festival and wants to invite several local cultural groups to perform. You have been given the task of writing an email to Atamai Latu, who used to go to your school and is a member of a Pacific Island performance group, asking if he, and his group, would perform at the International Festival.

Audience: the question has given you a specific person to write to — Atamai Latu. That means you can address him directly. Also, he is a former pupil so you can mention people and places he will know, such as your school's auditorium/hall.

Purpose: request and persuasion. You are asking him to take part in an event, so he will need all the relevant details. You are asking him for a favour, so you need to mention how grateful your/his old school will be.

The marker wants to see that you know how to use appropriate levels of formality in your writing.

There's a useful acronym you may know: **PIE**. *Persuade*, *Inform*, *Entertain*. These are the three overall purposes for a piece of writing.
You are unlikely to be asked to *Entertain* in this assessment, but you will be asked to *Persuade* or *Inform*.
The question will tell you your purpose, so read it carefully. It's as easy as PIE!

 ISBN: 9780170477581

Planning

A plan really helps you stay on track. It's worth taking a few minutes to think before you write.

First step: read

Read the question carefully.

The assessment will give the **audience** you are writing for by defining where the writing will be placed, like a newspaper, letter, magazine or blog, and so on. Note any key words that tell you for whom you are writing, words like: fellow students, parents, principal, mayor, community, and so on.

The assessment will also give you the **purpose** of your writing: persuading, informing, warning, complaining, and so on, by telling you what to write about. Note any key words that tell you the purpose of your writing, words like: explain, advise, describe, recommend, persuade, and so on.

You may have some choice about what you will write about within the topic. If this is the case, then select the written activity that you know most about or that relates most to your experience.

If there are words or pictures included in the question that suggest ideas to you, **use** them to:

- get your thinking started
- save time
- get organised.

Remember, they're there to help.

So, you have your topic and you have been given your writing task, and now you have to decide exactly what to write.

Second step: think

Once you have read the question and decided on the audience and the purpose, you will need more ideas, examples and details for your writing. You might be surprised by what you already know about the topic. Think about:

- personal experience
- information from a school subject like Science, Economics or Health/PE
- something that has happened in your family
- experiences of friends
- a place, event or activity in your community
- something you know about from the wider world
- things that you know from your hobbies
- other pieces of writing you have completed for school
- information you have read online or in a book.

ISBN: 9780170477581

Look at this **brainstorm** to see how a student thought about a topic before beginning to write.

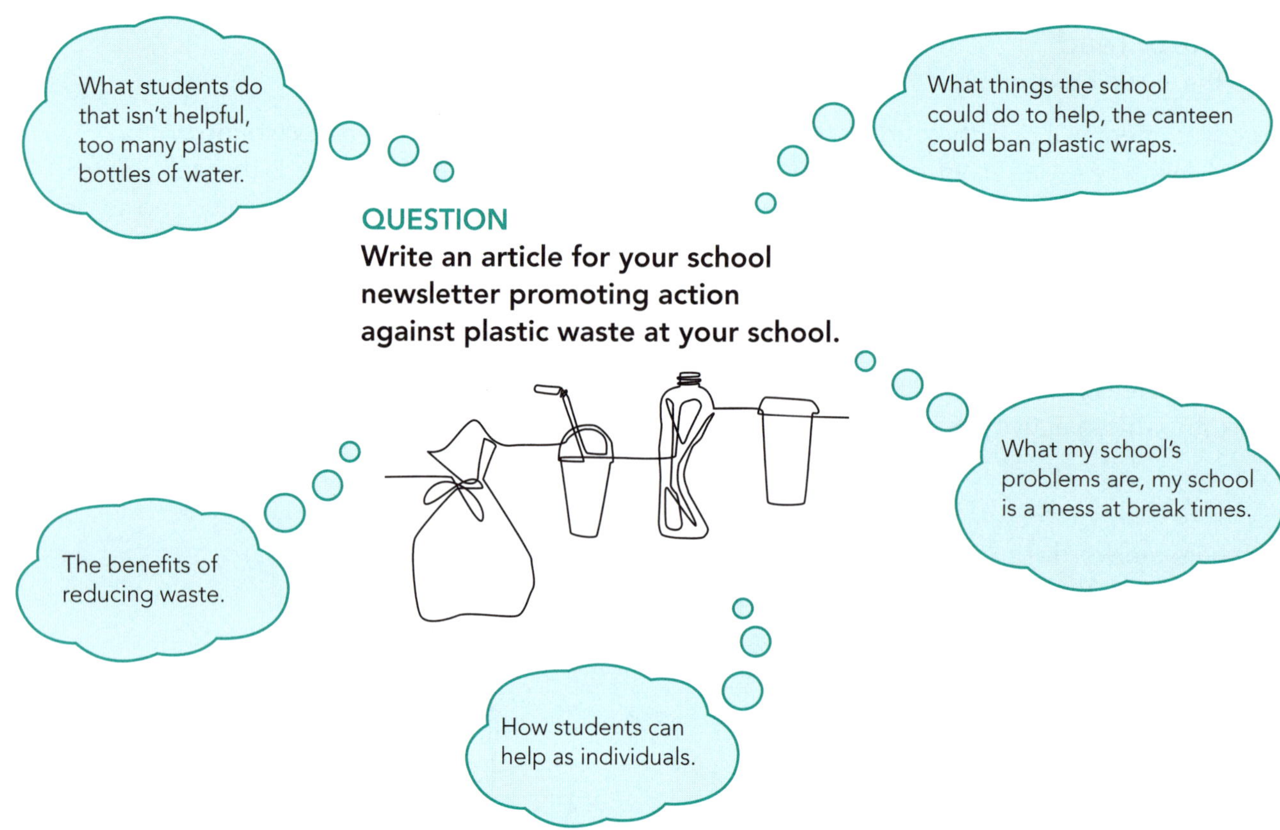

The student then added extra details from their studies and personal experience, like these:

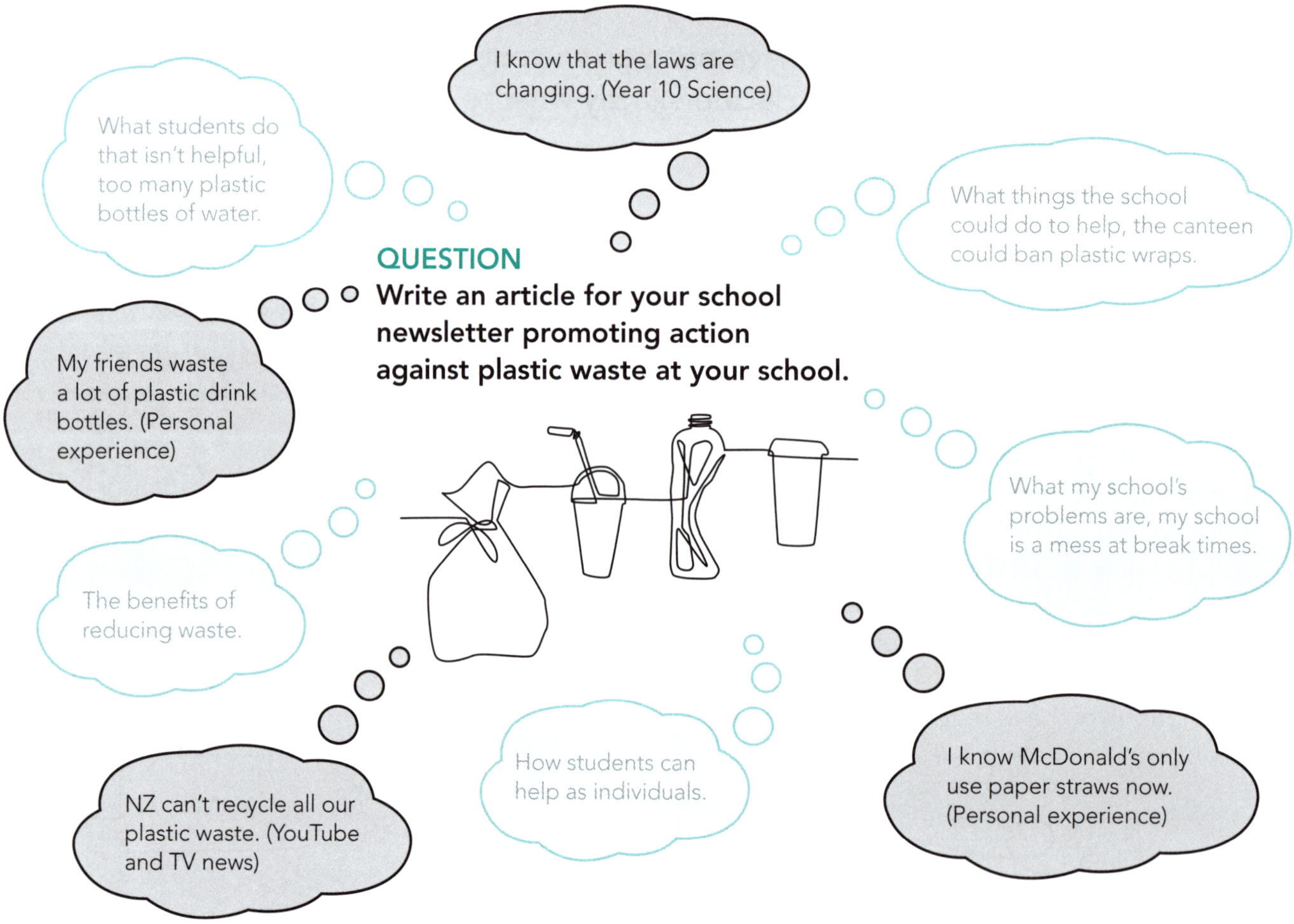

I know that the laws are changing. (Year 10 Science)

What students do that isn't helpful, too many plastic bottles of water.

What things the school could do to help, the canteen could ban plastic wraps.

QUESTION

Write an article for your school newsletter promoting action against plastic waste at your school.

My friends waste a lot of plastic drink bottles. (Personal experience)

What my school's problems are, my school is a mess at break times.

The benefits of reducing waste.

How students can help as individuals.

NZ can't recycle all our plastic waste. (YouTube and TV news)

I know McDonald's only use paper straws now. (Personal experience)

 ISBN: 9780170477581

Third step: plan

Now that you have had a chance to **brainstorm** and decide on some more detailed ideas and examples, you need to come up with a **plan** before you begin writing. Use the planning space to do the following:

- ***Note*** *your first ideas for your plan.*
- ***Add*** *examples, and any ideas from your own experience.*
- ***Organise*** *your ideas and examples into paragraphs on your plan.*
- ***Aim*** *for not too few, not too many ideas.*

The online assessment includes a space for you to plan. There is also a highlight and notes function that you may choose to use. When online, you can plan with bullet points or a list, which you can cut and paste to rearrange.

On paper you might use a graphic, a diagram, some doodles or just a list.

Do make a plan and then the actual writing will be easier.

Make sure you think and plan your writing. It will make you more efficient and make your writing more purposeful.

Structure

Organising your ideas into sentences and paragraphs

You have been writing in paragraphs for years. You may have learned this acronym or one similar:

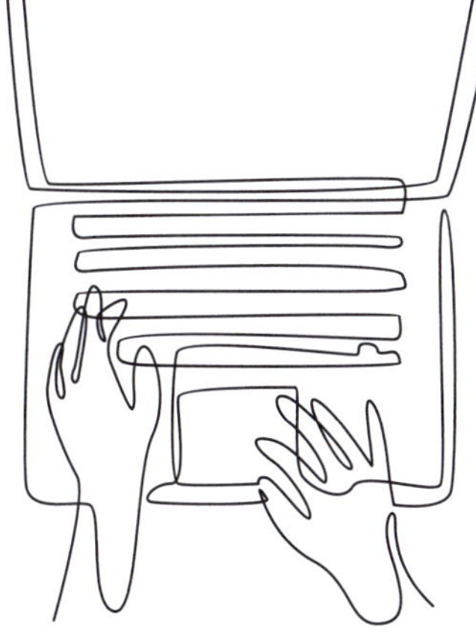

TEEC

- Topic
- Example
- Explanation
- Conclusion.

Following an acronym like this makes sure every paragraph is made of sentences that link together.

Then all you have to do is make sure the paragraphs are in a sequence that develops your thoughts from the opening statement to the concluding words of your piece of writing.

Here's an example of a student's paragraph on the same topic:

Write an article for your school newsletter promoting action against plastic waste at your school.

Our school is drowning in plastic, our own plastic.[T] The food sold in our school canteen is mostly wrapped in the plastic that is then dropped on the ground to blow through the corridors and across the field at the end of every break.[E] We accept this as normal even though no one wants to go out to pick it all up.[E] I believe it is time for us to stop this pollution of our environment by banning all food wrapped in plastic in our school canteen.[C]

Topic | Conclusion | Explanation | Example

ISBN: 9780170477581

The beginning and the end

For some students, starting and finishing a written piece is the hardest part of this assessment.

Here's a simple suggestion: **use the topic** and the **audience** and the **purpose** to guide how you begin and end the piece.

> **Write an article for your school newsletter promoting action against plastic waste at your school.**

Remember, you are promoting action against plastic waste to your fellow students in a newsletter.

Example:

Beginning: **New Zealand** has a huge **problem** with **plastic waste** and in our town and **our school** we must do something about this **today**.

Topic — plastic waste; Audience — our school; Purpose — do something about this today

End: We all know that **New Zealand** is making some effort to eliminate **plastic waste** but we students must all help by choosing only food *not* wrapped in **plastic** from our school canteen — starting tomorrow!

Topic — plastic waste; Audience — students; Purpose — choosing only food *not* wrapped in plastic

> **Advice**: if starting is really difficult for you, just leave a space and write the central paragraphs first. Add the opening when you've finished.

Writing to the required length

The next thing to focus on is how many words to write. This may sound unnecessary, but a lot of students don't write enough to pass this assessment and a few students write far too much on one answer and may not have time for the rest of the assessment.

Question: *How many words do you need to write for the longer piece?*

Answer: ***250 words as a minimum.***

You need to know before you take this test what 250 words looks like on the computer. It is important not to write too little and there isn't time to write too much.

ISBN: 9780170477581

Question: *How many words do you need to write for the shorter piece?*

Answer: ***150 words as a minimum.***

You need to know before you take this test what 150 words looks like on the computer. It is important not to write too little and there isn't time to write too much.

Some students find it very easy to write enough words, but for those who find it more challenging, here's some advice.

It's not rocket science, just common sense.

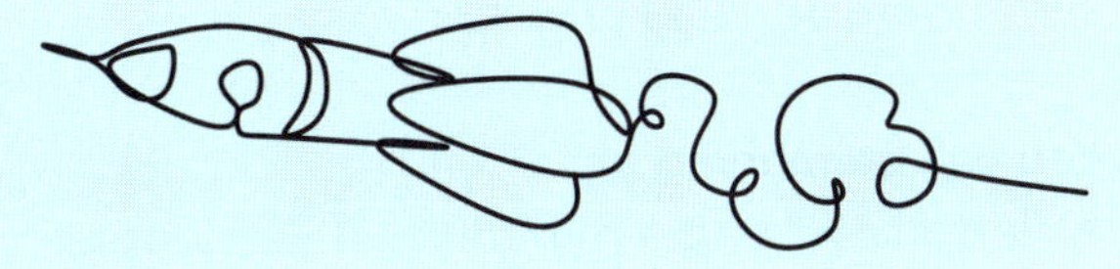

In a 250-word piece, six paragraphs should be enough. Let's say approximately 25 words for your introduction and 25 words for your conclusion. The remaining 200 words could be divided between four paragraphs, about 50 words per paragraph.

In a 150-word piece, four paragraphs may be enough. Let's say approximately 25 + 50 + 50 + 25 words.

Remember to leave a line between paragraphs, as this makes your words easier to read. If you check your practice writing for length, you will quickly be able to estimate how many words you have written without stopping to count up all the time.

If you are a one-finger typist, try the teach-yourself programs like Dance Mat Typing (from the BBC) or Typing Club to make typing faster and easier for you.

Checking your writing

An important part of the Writing assessment focuses on how accurately you can write. This includes your spelling, punctuation and grammar.

Technical errors interfere with the reader being able to understand what you have written. Just as with any piece of writing you do, in any subject, you need to take time to proofread your work. This includes using any spellcheck functions provided in the assessment. It isn't finished until you have done this.

It's important to read through your work. Reading aloud in your head does work because you will hear any major problems, like missing words. It is easy to miss your own mistakes, especially on the screen — try to read slowly and carefully.

It is *always* worth going back over your work to see if it is as accurate as you can make it.

Use this quick checklist every time you write anything. It will become routine the more you use it.

Quick check:

- Does it make sense?
- Is it long enough?
- Is it organised into paragraphs?
- Is there a capital letter at the start of every sentence?
- Is there a full stop at the end of every sentence?
- Does it say all I want to say on the topic?

ISBN: 9780170477581

Seeing is believing

Let's take a look at how a student organised their ideas in their own piece of writing.

QUESTION

Write an article for your school newsletter promoting action against plastic waste at your school.

Plan your writing, and check and edit your writing so it is clear for your reader.

Write between 250 and 350 words.

You will be marked on:

- length: writing a minimum of 250 words
- ideas: providing information and details that are appropriate for your audience and purpose
- structure: organising your ideas clearly and appropriately, with a clear beginning, middle and ending
- language choices: choosing words and sentences that are appropriate for your audience and purpose
- accuracy: using correct spelling, punctuation and grammar.

Student's brainstorm and plan

PLANNING

Who is my audience? School community (students, teachers, other staff, parents)

What is my purpose? To persuade people to stop using single-use plastic

Canteen apples in plastic wrap ... Water in plastic bottles ... Bananas own skin ... Plastic covers the ground after interval ... bins ... Ban the plastic bottle ... Start now ...

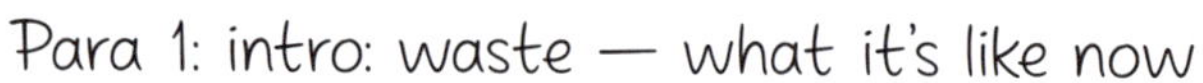

Para 1: intro: waste — what it's like now
Para 2: water bottles good idea
Para 3: canteen should stop selling plastic
Para 4: teachers can do it too, e.g. milk bottles in the staffroom, disposable coffee cups
Para 5: summary, small change to start

 ISBN: 9780170477581

Student's piece of writing

86 words. Statement of current situation.

Our school is drowning in plastic, our own plastic. The food sold in our school canteen is mostly wrapped in plastic that is then dropped on the ground to blow through the corridors and across the field at the end of every break. We accept this as normal even though no one wants to go out to pick it all up. I believe it is time for us to stop this pollution of our environment by banning all food wrapped in plastic in our school canteen.

43 words. Individual action suggestion.

All students should use reusable water bottles. We need water but we don't need every litre in a new throw-away bottle. Get one that you like, or use your mum's favourite one but use it every day for a year. I challenge you.

59 words. School rule action suggestion.

At school our canteen should sell nothing wrapped in plastic. That includes sandwiches, muffins and snacks. Fruit comes in eco-friendly wrapping, like bananas have their own skin and so do apples. Students can fill their water bottles at the drinking fountains rather than buy a new bottle of water at the canteen every day and then throw it away.

29 words. Teacher action suggestion.

Teachers can help too. If the milk for their tea and coffee came in glass bottles, not plastic ones, I think we'd reduce our plastic waste by a lot.

43 words. Call to begin action.

This is just a start but we can make a difference immediately by following these simple ideas. If everyone at our school makes a small change we can begin to reduce the plastic waste we see all around us at every break time.

Word count: 86 + 43 + 59 + 29 + 43 = 260. Just over the suggested the minimum word count.

The online assessment should have a word counter at the bottom of the page. Keep your eye on it. You need to meet the minimum, but you may exceed the maximum by a little.

12345678

Finally

You have been writing like this for years. You know how to do it!

Having read this section of the book, you have revised all the basics and you are ready to start practising for your Literacy Writing assessment. We will focus on three text types: letter, email and article. The help offered for these text types relates to any formal writing you will be asked to do.

How to write a formal letter

The Literacy assessment for Writing may ask you to write a formal letter. In the previous section of the book, we reminded you of the important basic skills for any formal writing (see pages 63–71), but there are specific techniques that we want to highlight when it comes to letter writing.

You might need to request information, present an idea or opinion to someone in a position of authority, or apply for a job or placement. All formal letters have the same features and follow a similar structure.

First think about:

your **audience**: who are you writing for?

and

your **purpose**: what are you are trying to achieve by writing your letter?

Who is your audience?

Look at the information within the topic question that you have been given and find any clues as to who you are writing to, such as what their position is. For example, in this assessment question you can see the name, role and company name of the person you will write to.

QUESTION

Write a letter to **Jamie Parata**, the **manager** of a local **New World supermarket**, thanking her for her store's donation to your sports team's participation in a national tournament in a different part of New Zealand.

What is your purpose?

You will be given a clear purpose for writing your letter. There may be some options within the question, so make sure you read it carefully. For example, in this assessment question you have been told the reason for you to write the letter.

QUESTION

Write a letter to Jamie Parata, the manager of a local New World supermarket, **thanking her for her store's donation** to your sports team's participation in a national tournament in a different part of New Zealand.

thank you

 ISBN: 9780170477581

Structure and organisation

- Letters follow a specific format. We have outlined the format in the example on the next page. It will help in the assessment if you are familiar with this structure.
- Formal letters begin with: *Heading*, *Dateline*, *Recipient Address*, *Salutation*. These are all shown in the example on the next page. It is usual to state your purpose in the opening sentence or sentences of your letter.
- The *Body* of your letter is where you write about the topic. It needs to be organised into paragraphs using well-constructed sentences. Think about topic sentences, explanatory sentences and examples. Page 74 has some guidelines.
- Formal letters end with a *Complimentary close*. See page 74 for an example.
- A successful letter supplies all the important information in a clear and concise manner.
- A *Writer's name and title* are typed following the *Complimentary close*. There is a gap left for the writer's signature.

Ideas

What shall I write? This type of assessment question might need you to use your imagination. Put yourself in the letter writer's place and think about what they might say.

- **What do I know?**

  You might not know a lot about the subject, but you can imagine yourself in the situation. In this example, at the very least, you need to think about which sport you, the letter writer, play. Where will the competition take place? What will the donation be used for? This assessment is about how well you write, not how factual you are. Be creative!

- **Stay focused on the topic.**

  This is important because it shows you have understood the question and can stay on topic, *but* don't repeat one idea three times. Again, be creative.

There is more advice on pages 65–67.

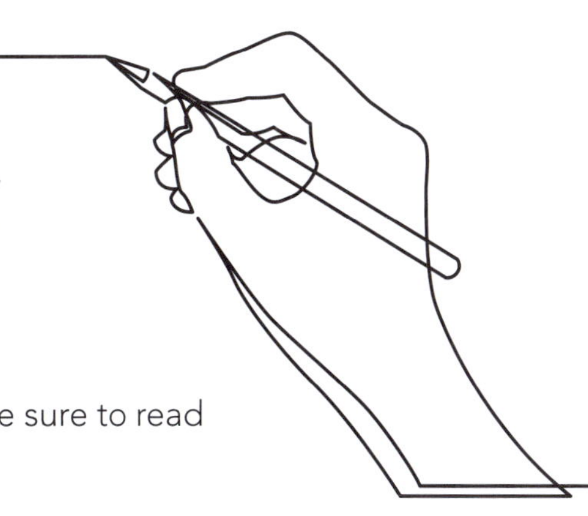

Language

Remember that a formal letter should not be written as if it is spoken, conversational English. Do not use slang or colloquialisms. Be polite, positive and very careful in expressing your ideas.

Check your letter

Part of this assessment is ensuring that you can write with accuracy. Be sure to read through your finished letter carefully. Here is some advice:

- Use the spell check if one is available.
- Check that you have written in complete sentences.
- See if your commas are in the right places.
- Look for misplaced or missing apostrophes.
- Make sure anything you copied from the question is correct.

We all make mistakes and you may be surprised at the number of simple errors you find that you can correct yourself. Make sure you read through our guidelines on page 69.

The basic structure of a formal letter

Follow this annotated example of a formal letter. It shows you the way to construct your own. It's easier to get the structure correct if you can 'see' your letter as a whole.

Heading
The *heading* of a letter is the address of the sender. In your assessment, you might include your home address, but it's fine to make one up.

Recipient address
The *recipient address* is the **name and address** of the person or business to whom you are sending the letter. Type the recipient address two lines under the dateline. This is sometimes called the *inside address*. Use the question prompts to get ideas about this. You can make up a street and numbers.

Dateline
When writing the *date*, the month should be written out in full, as should the year. The dateline should be typed or written two lines below the heading.

Salutation
A formal letter must begin with a formal greeting or *salutation*. You would usually use 'Dear (person's name)'. If you know their title (Dr, Ms, Mrs), use it. If you are unsure about title or gender, just use their first name.

36a Alexander Ave
Torbay
Auckland 0630

15 July 2024

New World Albany
219 Don McKinnon Drive
Albany
Auckland 0632

Dear Jamie,

Thank you for your kind donation of a $200 voucher to help our netball team raise funds for our upcoming national tournament in New Plymouth. Your support means a lot to us and we really appreciate your willingness to help us achieve our goal.

I am only 13 years old, so it's not easy to raise money for big events like this. Your contribution has made a big impact and has brought us a step closer to being able to cover the cost of food while we are away.

It is great to know that our community is supporting us as we represent our school and town at the national level. We hope that you will continue to support our team and other community groups in the future.

Thank you again for your kindness and generosity. We are grateful for your contribution to our netball team and look forward to seeing you in the store soon.

Yours sincerely,

Rebecca Moore

Rebecca Moore
Captain
Albany High School Junior Netball Squad

Complimentary close
The *complimentary close* is a courtesy signal at the end of your letter. Some good, professional choices are 'Yours sincerely,' or 'Yours faithfully,'. Never close a formal letter with 'Love,', 'Your friend,' or any other personal notation. The complimentary close should be typed two lines below the body of the letter.

Body
The *body* of the letter is where you write the letter to communicate your message. The body begins two lines below the salutation. In typing, the body paragraphs are usually single spaced with a line space between each paragraph. The body is the most important part of the letter. Think, plan, write in detail and check the body of the letter carefully.

Writer's name and title
The *writer's name* should be typed on the fourth line following the complimentary close. The space in between the complimentary close and the typed name is for the writer's signature. Use your own or make one up.

ISBN: 9780170477581

How to write a formal email

As an alternative to a letter, you may be asked to write an email.

This doesn't mean you can dash off a quick chatty message on social media or email like you would to your friends and family. You will be given your audience and your purpose in the assessment question, just like for a full formal letter. It may be a person you do not know or someone in authority, like your principal, that you do know. Just like the formal letter, you will need to choose more formal language.

Always use language that is appropriate for your audience and your purpose.

The basic structure of an email

Follow this annotated example of an email. It shows you the way to construct your own email. It is easy to get this structure correct if you can 'see' your email as a whole.

If the date, time, email address, and so on isn't provided in the assessment question, make up logical ones from the information you have been given.

From
Your email address will show on an actual email. You may use your own or an imaginary one.

Date and time
When sending a real email, the computer creates the email's date and time sent. However, you will need to create them in this assessment.

To
The recipient's email address.

Subject line
The subject line in an email signposts for the recipient what the email is about.

Salutation
A formal email uses the same sort of salutation as the formal letter. Do not use 'Hey there!' in a formal email.

From: m.thomas12871@nphs.school.nz
Date: 11 April 2024 at 4.40 pm
To: Peters.Lily@gmail.com
Cc:
Subject: Stage Challenge Crew — School Auditorium Booking

Dear Mrs Peters

I wanted to inform you that the Stage Challenge Crew has booked the school auditorium every Wednesday between 3.15 and 5 pm for the next two months. We will be using the auditorium for rehearsals leading up to the Stage Challenge competition.

Mrs Anderton has agreed to oversee the group during these rehearsals and the Performing Arts prefects will also be present to assist with supervision.

We understand that the auditorium is an essential space for many school activities and we appreciate the opportunity to use this facility for our rehearsals. We assure you that we will take great care in using the auditorium and will leave it in the same condition as we found it.

Thank you for your support.

Mackenzie Thomas
Head Performing Arts Prefect

Cc
This means carbon copy. If the email is copied to another person, their email address goes here. Carbon copy means an exact copy of this email is sent to another person, and the main recipient is able to see that it has been sent to that person.

Body of email
The body of the email is where you write about the purpose of the email. The body begins two lines below the salutation. See the information for the body of a letter on page 74. An email may be shorter, but it's the same in principle. Use paragraphs.

Writer's name and title
You should end your email with your name and role (if appropriate). You may be given your role in the assessment question information. If not, you may make up a logical one.

Complimentary close
The complimentary close is a courtesy signal at the end of your email. Some good, professional choices are 'Yours sincerely,' or 'Yours faithfully,'. Never close a formal email with 'Love,', 'Your friend,' or any other personal notation.

Task 1: Formal letter

The best way to improve at writing letters is to write letters. Let's begin with an example of a student's response to a question that says **write a letter**. Students were given the following assessment question.

QUESTION

As part of their Year 11 PE course, students had to attend a three-day adventure camp to experience a range of outdoor education activities.

Write a letter thanking Roger Davies, the owner of The Great Outdoors Adventure Camp, for hosting the class and explaining what you liked about the camp.

Plan your writing, and check and edit your writing so it is clear for your reader.

Write between 250 and 350 words.

You will be marked on:

- length: writing a minimum of 250 words
- ideas: providing information and details that are appropriate for your audience and purpose
- structure: organising your ideas clearly and appropriately, with a clear beginning, middle and ending
- language choices: choosing words and sentences that are appropriate for your audience and purpose
- accuracy: using correct spelling, punctuation and grammar.

Now take a look at the planning and letter the student wrote.

PLANNING

Audience: Roger and his staff at The Great Outdoors Adventure Camp.
Purpose: To thank them for our stay.

Liked the food, especially the burgers
Lots of activities that we rotated around
Liked mountain biking and the flying fox
Became more confident
Home cooking was good, lots of choices
Went on a glowworm trip on a boat
Learnt about the different safety procedures
Was good for our assessment because now we have lots of examples
Liked learning about the native bush

Paragraph on:

- food
- what activities
- what I learned at camp
- thank them for their time and effort

Some words I could use:

enjoyment
fantastic
information
knowledge
skills

ISBN: 9780170477581

STUDENT'S WORK

5 Rata Place
Tui Glen
Hamilton 3291

15 May 2024

The Great Outdoors Adventure Camp
Kaka Park
RD 3
Hamilton

Dear Roger,

I am writing this letter to thank you for the fantastic three-day camp that our Year 11 PE class had at The Great Outdoors Adventure Camp. I think that we all enjoyed every moment of it.

Firstly, the food was amazing, especially the burgers. Everyone ate everything at meal times so the cooks were brilliant at feeding us food we would like. All the snacks were great, too. We didn't even mind doing the washing up!

Secondly, the activities were fantastic, and we all had a great time trying out every option. My favourite activities were the mountain biking and the flying fox. The bike track was really hard but I got better at it and the flying fox was seriously scary. I also enjoyed the night-time boat trip to see the glowworms.

Also, the camp has helped us with our confidence because we had to try new things. We had to be careful with setting up activities safely and I'm sure we will all think about being more responsible for ourselves and for each other in the outdoors now. We also learned more about the New Zealand bush and how special it is.

Lastly, the camp gave us plenty of information to help with our upcoming Outdoor Education assessment. We will be able to write about our environment and the safety skills we learnt at camp.

I want to say thank you for a brilliant experience. I appreciate all the effort that went into giving us such a great time.

Yours sincerely,

Kelly Winiata

Kelly Winiata
Year 11 PE Student
Clifton College

YOUR TURN

You have read the plan and the letter written by the student. Complete the following activities.

1 Annotate the *Heading*, *Dateline*, *Recipient address*, *Salutation*, *Body*, *Complimentary close* and *Writer's name and title*.
2 Use different-coloured highlighters to match the ideas from the plan that go together well *and* where those ideas are used in the letter.
3 Count the words. Is it long enough?
4 Count the paragraphs. How many?
5 Highlight the start of each paragraph. Note how these opening words can help a student to structure the letter.
6 Highlight detailed information the student has created to make the letter seem real.

Imagine you are in the same Year 11 PE class. Plan and write your own thank you letter on a separate piece of paper. You may use some of Kelly's structure, but try to add ideas and examples of your own.

ISBN: 9780170477581

Task 2: Formal email

You will be asked to write a shorter piece, too. This may be in the form of an email. Here is a possible question.

QUESTION

As part of your school's short-term exchange programme with its sister school in Tagikawa, Japan, you will be hosting a student in your home for a term. Your student, whose name is Aki, will have a reasonable knowledge of English and will be attending some classes with you. They are here to practise conversational English and learn about our way of living and culture.

Write an email introducing yourself, your school and/or your community.

Plan your writing, and check and edit your writing so it is clear for your reader.

Write between 150 and 250 words.

You will be marked on:

- length: writing a minimum of 150 words
- ideas: providing information and details that are appropriate for your audience and purpose
- structure: organising your ideas clearly and appropriately, with a clear beginning, middle and ending
- language choices: choosing words and sentences that are appropriate for your audience and purpose
- accuracy: using correct spelling, punctuation and grammar.

In the planning box, we have included a few suggestions, but you should make more plans for yourself.

PLANNING

Who is my audience? ______________________

What is my purpose? ______________________

Think about:
Introduce myself and my family
I'm learning Japanese. Manga
Describe where I live
Uniform Years 7–11. Colour. Comfort?
Language differences, Māori words in NZ English: pā, marae, kia ora

THINK: what do I know about this topic?

 ISBN: 9780170477581

TIME TO WRITE

From

Date and time

To

Cc

Subject

Salutation

Body

Complimentary close

Writer's name and title

If you are writing by hand, you may have to add extra refill pages. If you are typing your writing on a computer rather than in this book, then printing the page is a good idea.

CHECK YOUR WORK

- Have I got names from the question right?
- Is it long enough?
- Is it organised into paragraphs?
- Is there a capital letter at the start of every sentence?
- Is there a full stop at the end of every sentence?
- Is my spelling okay? Have I used any available spellchecker?
- Does it say all I want to say on the topic?

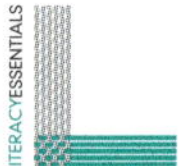

Task 3: Formal letter

You may be asked to write a letter of application. Students often find this quite difficult because it can be hard to 'sell' ourselves. Here is a possible question asking you to apply for a position and a way of approaching it.

QUESTION

Your local pet shop, Pets Are for Life, is advertising in the local newspaper for a school student to help out with animal care on Sundays. This will be your first paid employment. Write the letter that you will send to the shop to apply for the role.

Plan your writing, and check and edit your writing so it is clear for your reader.

Write between 150 and 250 words.

You will be marked on:

- length: writing a minimum of 150 words
- ideas: providing information and details that are appropriate for your audience and purpose
- structure: organising your ideas clearly and appropriately, with a clear beginning, middle and ending
- language choices: choosing words and sentences that are appropriate for your audience and purpose
- accuracy: using correct spelling, punctuation and grammar.

PLANNING

Who is my audience? ______________________________

What is my purpose? ______________________________

Think about:

THINK: what do I know about this topic?

- why you are interested in the job
- what experience you have with animals
- what skills you have that would suit the job
- why you hope the store owner will give you an interview.

Use positive words like 'I can', 'I have', 'I will', and so on.
Be enthusiastic!
Remember to ask the store owner to contact you.

 ISBN: 9780170477581

TIME TO WRITE

CHECK YOUR WORK

- Have I got names from the question right?
- Is it long enough?
- Is it organised into paragraphs?
- Is there a capital letter at the start of every sentence?
- Is there a full stop at the end of every sentence?
- Is my spelling okay? Have I used any available spellchecker?
- Does it say all I want to say on the topic?

If you are writing by hand, you may have to add extra refill pages. If you are typing your writing on a computer rather than in this book, then printing the page is a good idea.

How to write an article

The Literacy assessment for Writing may ask you to write an article. An article can be published in a newspaper, a newsletter, a magazine or similar communications, which might be in print form and/or on the internet.

You will be given the topic and suggestions about what to include in your article in the assessment question. It will be a topic that students could be expected to know something about, but you may need to be inventive.

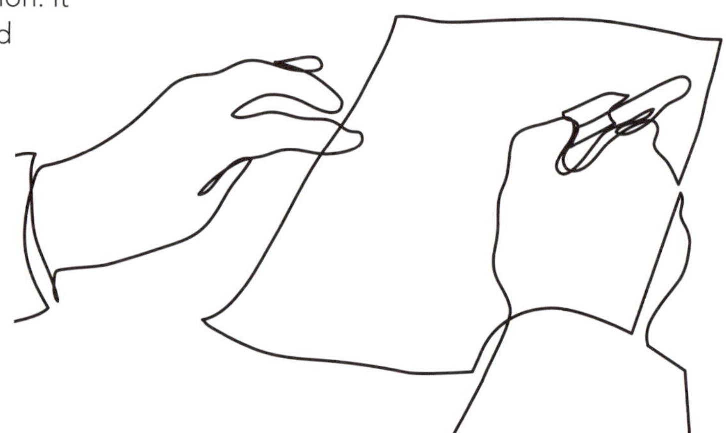

As we have said before, first think about:

your **audience**: who are you writing for?

and

your **purpose**: what are you trying to achieve through writing your article?

Who is your audience?

Look at the information within the question and find any clues as to where your article is going to be published. For example, in the assessment question below the audience has been clearly identified as people linked to your school community. That means your article should relate to things in your school community.

> **QUESTION**
> Write an article for your school newsletter for **parents and caregivers** about the new recycling system that you and your Sustainability Team of students are introducing.

What is your purpose?

You will be given a clear purpose for writing your article. There may be some options within the question, so make sure you read it carefully. In this assessment question you have been told the topic of the article.

> **QUESTION**
> Write an article for your school newsletter for parents and caregivers about the **new recycling system that you and your Sustainability Team of students are introducing**.

You might state your purpose in the opening sentence or sentences of your article.

 ISBN: 9780170477581

Structure and organisation

There are five parts to an article: headline, byline, lead sentence, body and closing sentence.

The **headline** needs to catch the reader's attention. It is usually short, snappy and informative. It will often include alliteration or word play. However, don't spend too much of your assessment time working on a headline.

The **byline** is the name of the writer — your name, in this case.

The **lead sentence** should give the key information — Who? What? Where? When? The first sentence is often the most important one, as it is needs to grab the reader's attention and interest them to read on.

The **body of your article** includes all the relevant facts and details that relate to your lead sentence — the Why? and How? This could also include additional information that might help the reader learn more, additional facts about the topic or people involved or quotes from interviews. These help to round out the article.

You finish with a good **closing sentence**. It could restate the lead sentence, offer some thoughts for the future, ask a question, suggest an action.

When you are planning, think about:

Who was involved?
What happened?
Where did it happen?
When did it happen?
Why did it happen?
How did it happen?

Ideas

What shall I write? This type of assessment question might need you to use your imagination. Put yourself in the writer's place and think about what they might say.

- **What do I know?**

  You might not know a lot about the subject, so you may need to be inventive. This assessment is about how well you write, not how factual you are.
  Be creative!

- **Stay focused on the topic.**

  This is important because it shows you have understood the question and can stay on topic, *but* don't repeat one idea three times.
  Again, be creative.

There is more advice on pages 65–67.

ISBN: 9780170477581

Language

When you write an article for the Literacy assessment you need to demonstrate that you respect your readers and that you are treating your subject matter seriously. Here is some advice:

- Remember that an article should not be too personal.
- Maintain a formal style while still being engaging.
- Do not use chatty, conversational English.
- Use straightforward vocabulary.
- Use third person pronouns (he, she, it, they).
- Write in the past tense if the events have already happened.

Confident use of formal English here demonstrates that you understand that we use English differently in different situations.

Check your article

Part of this assessment is ensuring that you can write with accuracy. Be sure to read through your finished article carefully. Here is some advice:

- Use the spell check if one is available.
- Check that you have written in complete sentences.
- See if your commas are in the right places.
- Look for misplaced or missing apostrophes.
- Make sure anything you copied from the question is correct.

We all make mistakes and you may be surprised at the number of simple errors you find that you can correct yourself.

Make sure you read through our guidelines on page 69.

ISBN: 9780170477581

The basic structure of an article

Follow this annotated example of an article. It shows you the way to construct your own.

Headline: short, states topic clearly.

Lead sentence gives the big picture, followed by key information.

Recycling Made Easy

Our new recycling system

The issue of climate change is affecting everyone on our planet, and it is becoming important that we all do our part to protect the environment. In an effort to make our school more environmentally friendly, our Sustainability Team is introducing a new recycling system at the beginning of Term 2 that will make it easy for students, teachers and other staff to recycle materials.

Repetition of 'recycling' at start of each body paragraph keeps writer on track.

The new recycling system involves four bins in each classroom: yellow, blue, green and red. The yellow bin is for recycling plastic, cans and glass, while the blue bin is for recycling paper. The green bin is for recycling organic materials, and the red bin is for non-recyclable rubbish.

Recycling is important because it reduces the amount of waste that goes into landfills and helps to look after natural resources. When we recycle, we are saving energy, reducing pollution, and helping to create a more sustainable future for ourselves and future generations.

Body gives more details. On Where? On How? On Why?

In conclusion, by introducing this new recycling system, we hope to encourage everyone in our school community to take responsibility for their waste and to recycle materials whenever possible. We are all responsible for protecting the environment, and recycling is an easy and effective way to do so.

Positive words: easy, important, helps, encourage, protecting, effective, greener.

Let's work together to protect our planet and make our school a greener place.

by Henry Orchard

Closing sentence suggests a positive, inclusive action to the reader.

Byline

5Ws, 1H

- Who? The Sustainability Team, students, all staff
- What? New recycling system implemented
- Where? At a school
- Why? To reduce the waste going into landfills
- When? The beginning of Term 2
- How? Various different bins in classrooms

Task 4: Article

Let's begin with an example of a student's response to a question that says **write an article**. Students were given the following assessment question.

QUESTION

Write an article for your school newsletter about the benefits of joining an extra-curricular activity while you are at high school.

Plan your writing, and check and edit your writing so it is clear for your reader.

Write between 250 and 350 words.

You will be marked on:

- length: writing a minimum of 250 words
- ideas: providing information and details that are appropriate for your audience and purpose
- structure: organising your ideas clearly and appropriately, with a clear beginning, middle and ending
- language choices: choosing words and sentences that are appropriate for your audience and purpose
- accuracy: using correct spelling, punctuation and grammar.

Now take a look at the planning for the article that the student wrote.

PLANNING

Audience: Students, teachers and parents in your school community

Purpose: What is good about doing an extra-curricular activity

Kapa haka, drama, choir, kī-o-rahi, computer gaming, cricket, touch, netball, art, chess, grow your own food, culture club, debating, orchestra

Exercising body and brain

Meet people from other cultures

Do what I'm good at

Learn how to do things

Get involved in school more

Gaining skills for life

Paragraph on:

1 Choices

2 Improving skills

3 New skills

4 New people

5 My choices.

 ISBN: 9780170477581

STUDENT'S WORK

Join a club — I dare you!

At school we don't have a lot of choice about what we do in class. English, Maths and Science is for everyone but extra-curricular activities you can choose for yourself. Here at Clifton College there are lots of choices: sports, music, computers and drama — and that's just on Wednesdays.

Extra-curricular activities can help you improve your skills in areas you already know you are interested in. You might play an instrument but want to learn another. Join the orchestra. You might sing in the shower at home but at school you can join a choir and learn how to perform properly.

Also, extra-curricular activities can help you find new interests and strengths. You might have always wanted to try acting but felt too shy. Joining the Acting Club can get you started. Or try chess, or computer gaming with people who can help you develop basic skills. Extra-curricular activities like these can exercise your brain, or try a new sport to exercise your body.

In school we have our classmates but joining an extra-curricular activity means you will meet new people, students (and even teachers) who like the same things as you do and who you might never meet unless you try something new. You can get to know people from different year levels and from other cultures too if you join a club and get involved.

I have been in lots of different clubs at school. It's great to be involved and I feel part of the whole school community because I've been in representative teams like for touch and also small groups like the Horticulture Grower's Club. My advice to you is to JOIN A CLUB. Get involved and get the most out of school.

by Mari Purnett

YOUR TURN

You have read the plan and the article written by the student. Complete the following activities.

1 Annotate the 5Ws and 1H in this article.
2 Use different-coloured highlighters to match the ideas from the plan that go together well *and* where those ideas are used in the article.
3 Count the words. Is it long enough?
4 Count the paragraphs. How many?
5 Highlight the start of each paragraph. Note how these opening words introduce the topic.
6 Highlight detailed information the student has created to make the article seem real.

Imagine you have been asked to write the same article for your school newsletter. Plan and write your own article on a separate piece of paper. You may use some of Mari's structure, but try to add ideas and examples of your own.

ISBN: 9780170477581

Task 5: Article

Here is a possible question asking you to write an article about ideas people your age might have. You may need to be inventive if you have never thought about community gardens before.

QUESTION

Mrs Philips, a teacher at your local primary school, has asked your Year 11 Agriculture class to help with some ideas about starting a community garden at their school. Your class comes up with some good ideas. Write an article for your school newsletter summarising the ideas.

Plan your writing, and check and edit your writing so it is clear for your reader.

Write between 250 and 350 words.

You will be marked on:
- length: writing a minimum of 250 words
- ideas: providing information and details that are appropriate for your audience and purpose
- structure: organising your ideas clearly and appropriately, with a clear beginning, middle and ending
- language choices: choosing words and sentences that are appropriate for your audience and purpose
- accuracy: using correct spelling, punctuation and grammar.

PLANNING

Who is my audience? ______________________________

What is my purpose? ______________________________

THINK: what do I know about this topic?

Think about the 5Ws and 1H:
- Why your class thought it was a great idea.
- Where is a good location for the garden?
- When is the best time to plant?
- What to grow?
- Who will get the plants?
- How to organise the gardening.

TIME TO WRITE

____

____

____

____

____

____

____

 ISBN: 9780170477581

If you are writing by hand, you may have to add extra refill pages. If you are typing your writing on a computer rather than in this book, then printing the page is a good idea.

CHECK YOUR WORK

- Have I got names from the question right?
- Is it long enough?
- Is it organised into paragraphs?
- Is there a capital letter at the start of every sentence?
- Is there a full stop at the end of every sentence?
- Is my spelling okay? Have I used any available spellchecker?
- Does it say all I want to say on the topic?

Task 6: Article

Here is another possible question that requires you to write an article. Sometimes you may need to invent material for your writing. We have given you some ideas in the planning section to help you get started with your own planning.

QUESTION

The local youth centre is running a competition for ideas for a mural on the outside wall of the centre. The only criterion is that the mural must have something with local significance.

Write a newspaper article for your community newsletter about the competition. You may need to use your imagination a little.

Plan your writing, and check and edit your writing so it is clear for your reader.

Write between 250 and 350 words.

You will be marked on:

- length: writing a minimum of 250 words
- ideas: providing information and details that are appropriate for your audience and purpose
- structure: organising your ideas clearly and appropriately, with a clear beginning, middle and ending
- language choices: choosing words and sentences that are appropriate for your audience and purpose
- accuracy: using correct spelling, punctuation and grammar.

In the planning box, we have included a few planning words, but you should make more plans for yourself.

PLANNING

Who is my audience? ______________________________

What is my purpose? ______________________________

Think about:

THINK: what do I know about this topic?

- Wall is plain, boring
- Wanting to brighten up building
- Avoid graffiti
- Competition details
- What might teenagers like?

 ISBN: 9780170477581

TIME TO WRITE

CHECK YOUR WORK

- Have I got names from the question right?
- Is it long enough?
- Is it organised into paragraphs?
- Is there a capital letter at the start of every sentence?
- Is there a full stop at the end of every sentence?
- Is my spelling okay? Have I used any available spellchecker?
- Does it say all I want to say on the topic?

If you are writing by hand, you may have to add extra refill pages. If you are typing your writing on a computer rather than in this book, then printing the page is a good idea.

ISBN: 9780170477581

What else might you have to write?

In this book, we have focused on formal letter/email and article writing, but there are many other text types that you might be asked to write. We have outlined some of the possible options below. We have also included an example of the type of question you might be asked for each of these text types. For more writing practice, take any or all of these questions and write an answer of 150 words or more. After all, practice makes perfect! The good news is that by now you have a very good understanding of the key features of formal writing and can apply them to any style.

Whatever you are asked to write, keep the same things in mind:

- Who is the audience?
- Use structure and paragraphs.
- What is the purpose?
- Use appropriate language.

Don't forget … it's as easy as **PIE**!

Online forum, blog or social media post

You likely read the most while you are online, so there is a good chance the assessment might ask you to write something that would be published online.

You might be tempted to think that if you are asked to write something online that you can be more casual in your structure and language choice. However, in most cases, your work will still end up in a public setting and so you need to ensure you apply the rules of formal structure and are respectful in your language.

The exception to this might be if you are asked to write something to someone your own age — if this is the case, stop and think: where is this being published? Who else might read it? If it is more of a public forum, then you will definitely have to think formally even though you have been asked to write to someone of your own age.

QUESTION

Your school is promoting walking or cycling to school to help the environment. However, your year group is not happy about the access to your school's front entrance.

Write a blog post for your school's website that explains what you believe needs to be done to keep students safe as they walk or cycle to school.

You might mention footpaths, bike paths, traffic speed zone, pedestrian crossing, etc. Be inventive if you need to.

Opinion piece

You might get asked for your opinion on an issue, event or person. Just because it is your thoughts doesn't mean that you get to write it in quite the same manner as you would speak it to a friend. You will need to think about how you can present your ideas with an appropriate tone, especially if you feel negatively about the issue, event or person. You are entitled to your opinion, but no one wants to read anything that is rude.

You may have written an essay or report on an issue as part of your English, Social Studies or even Science classes. Use what you have learnt and apply it to this type of writing.

Focus on structure, making sure you use an introduction, body and conclusion. Your body paragraphs should follow our TEEC structure from page 67.

Make sure you explain your opinion while backing up what you have said with clear concise information — you may need to invent this information/evidence.

QUESTION

Teenagers use social media a lot for writing about their personal lives. Is this a good or bad thing?

Write an item for your local youth group's newsletter giving your opinion about what is good for teenagers to share online and what is not.

You might mention things that should be private like personal information (address or phone number) as opposed to public things like holiday photographs or opinions about movies or books.

Review

You might be asked to write a review. This is similar to an opinion piece in that it is *your* opinion, but, again, even if you didn't like something, you need to be respectful to the person who created it.

Potentially, the assessment could ask you to review a film, a book, a concert or perhaps a restaurant you visited recently.

Structure is important. You should make clear in the introduction if your overall opinion is positive or negative.

Then in your body paragraphs, explain why you hold this opinion, making sure you have evidence to back it up. Remember that this can be made-up evidence.

You should also use emotive language to try to really get your opinion across, for instance, you might try to get your reader excited to go to see the film because you think it's awesome!

QUESTION

Your school library has a noticeboard where students can display reviews of books they have read or movies they have seen or video games they have played.

Write a review of a book or movie or game that you have enjoyed for this noticeboard, encouraging other people to read/see/play it.

You might write about the plot, characters, action, ideas, skill, etc. It is best to use a real example that you have read, seen or played but you may invent one if you are able to do so.

Report or explanation

A report is usually about something you have seen, heard, done or investigated. Again, you may have written something similar in Science, English or Social Studies.

Be sure to read all of the information given to you in the question, as it will help you. Structure is important as is using information to back up what you are saying. If you aren't given the information, make it up, but try to make it believable.

ISBN: 9780170477581

An explanation is similar to a report in that you could be explaining something you have seen or heard or done. However, it could also be that you need to explain a process. You might be asked to explain how to soft boil an egg to someone, or how to get a bus to the mall.

If you are describing a process, make sure you progress from start to finish in a logical sequence. Read the question carefully to make sure you understand exactly what it is asking you to explain.

QUESTION

The students in your school suffer from hot classrooms during the summer terms and cold classrooms during winter terms.

As the representative of your class, write a letter to the Board of Trustees about installing heat pumps in all classrooms. Explain why it would be helpful to improve the temperature and air quality in classrooms.

You might mention comfort, concentration, achievement in tests, health, absenteeism, even smells, etc.

Profile of a person

This type of writing might ask you to nominate someone you know to win a competition or award such as TVNZ's Good Sorts, or you might be asked to write an article to describe a role model you have.

You need to follow whichever format you have been asked to write in and then also think how best to promote your chosen person. This is persuasive writing, but is more personal.

It is a good idea to think about who you would pick from your life, and why, *before* you go into the assessment. That way you can have some ideas ready to tap into if a question like this comes up.

Think about someone who has had a positive impact on your life. It will likely be someone older than you, perhaps a family member, a coach, a teacher or a senior student, but it could be a teammate or a friend. Once you've decided who, then try to pinpoint two or three things that make them that person for you. These will be the ideas you will develop into paragraphs.

QUESTION

'Youth Parliament is held every three years, and is a unique opportunity for young New Zealanders to learn first-hand about our democracy, influence government decision-making, and have their voices heard.'

You would like to nominate a person in your class to represent your school at the Youth Parliament. Write your nomination in an email to your school principal that explains why that student would be the ideal representative of your school.

You might mention the person's interest in politics, involvement in the school council, running events at school, concern for others, etc.

In all cases, whatever you are asked to write, you need to consider that it is a formal piece of writing, which has a beginning, middle and end. It is not a chat to your friends over a pizza!

ISBN: 9780170477581

Let's practise

QUESTION 1

Your local recreation place (beach, park, sport courts, riverside, and so on) has been neglected and it is no longer a place for the community to enjoy spending time there. You are part of the Environmental Group at your school, which wants to suggest to the local council that the recreation place needs improving. The group has some ideas as to what could be done to improve the area.

Write a letter to the mayor asking for your chosen area to be improved and outline your group's suggestions.

Plan your writing, and check and edit your writing so it is clear for your reader.

Write between 250 and 350 words.

You will be marked on:

- length: writing a minimum of 250 words
- ideas: providing information and details that are appropriate for your audience and purpose
- structure: organising your ideas clearly and appropriately, with a clear beginning, middle and ending
- language choices: choosing words and sentences that are appropriate for your audience and purpose
- accuracy: using correct spelling, punctuation and grammar.

PLANNING

Who is my audience? ______________________________

What is my purpose? ______________________________

Think about:

THINK: what do I know about this topic?

- What the area is and what your group thinks is wrong with the area now.
- What could be done to improve the place.
- What the benefits of improving the area are.
- What you and your group are prepared to do to help.

Remember all the advice about planning and structuring a letter (pages 72–74).

 ISBN: 9780170477581

TIME TO WRITE

CHECK YOUR WORK

- Have I got names from the question right?
- Is it long enough?
- Is it organised into paragraphs?
- Is there a capital letter at the start of every sentence?
- Is there a full stop at the end of every sentence?
- Is my spelling okay? Have I used any available spellchecker?
- Does it say all I want to say on the topic?

If you are writing by hand, you may have to add extra refill pages. If you are typing your writing on a computer rather than in this book, then printing the page is a good idea.

 ISBN: 9780170477581

QUESTION 2

Yesterday, your school held a one-day cultural festival. This event celebrated the ethnically diverse, multicultural nature of your school. There were food stalls and performances by many different cultures, and lots of parents were involved. It was a huge success.

Today, you have been asked to write an article for the local newspaper about this event.

Plan your writing, and check and edit your writing so it is clear for your reader.

Write between 250 and 350 words.

You will be marked on:

- length: writing a minimum of 250 words
- ideas: providing information and details that are appropriate for your audience and purpose
- structure: organising your ideas clearly and appropriately, with a clear beginning, middle and ending
- language choices: choosing words and sentences that are appropriate for your audience and purpose
- accuracy: using correct spelling, punctuation and grammar.

PLANNING

Who is my audience? ______________________________

What is my purpose? ______________________________

Think about:

THINK: what do I know about this topic?

- Who organised the festival.
- Which countries were represented and by whom.
- How colourful the costumes and clothing were.
- How tasty the food was.
- Some responses from student attendees and/or staff.

Remember all the advice about planning and structuring an article (pages 82–85).

ISBN: 9780170477581

TIME TO WRITE

ISBN: 9780170477581

CHECK YOUR WORK

- Have I got names from the question right?
- Is it long enough?
- Is it organised into paragraphs?
- Is there a capital letter at the start of every sentence?
- Is there a full stop at the end of every sentence?
- Is my spelling okay? Have I used any available spellchecker?
- Does it say all I want to say on the topic?

If you are writing by hand, you may have to add extra refill pages. If you are typing your writing on a computer rather than in this book, then printing the page is a good idea.

QUESTION 3

Your school has decided to ban the use of cellphones during the school day. You agree with this decision and wish to explain why, with some personal observations. Write an email to your principal explaining why you support the decision to ban cellphones during the school day.

Plan your writing, and check and edit your writing so it is clear for your reader.

Write between 150 and 250 words.

You will be marked on:

- length: writing a minimum of 150 words
- ideas: providing information and details that are appropriate for your audience and purpose
- structure: organising your ideas clearly and appropriately, with a clear beginning, middle and ending
- language choices: choosing words and sentences that are appropriate for your audience and purpose
- accuracy: using correct spelling, punctuation and grammar.

PLANNING

Who is my audience? ______________________________

What is my purpose? ______________________________

Some words and phrases you could think about:

THINK: what do I know about this topic?

- distracting
- disturbing concentration
- face to face better
- cyber bullying
- competitive.

Remember all the advice about planning and structuring an email (page 75).

 ISBN: 9780170477581

TIME TO WRITE

If you are writing by hand, you may have to add extra refill pages. If you are typing your writing on a computer rather than in this book, then printing the page is a good idea.

CHECK YOUR WORK

- Have I got names from the question right?
- Is it long enough?
- Is it organised into paragraphs?
- Is there a capital letter at the start of every sentence?
- Is there a full stop at the end of every sentence?
- Is my spelling okay? Have I used any available spellchecker?
- Does it say all I want to say on the topic?

QUESTION 4

You are part of a group of students who are organising a donation drive at your school to support either:

- **Jammies for June**

  or

- **Can Drive for a local food bank.**

Your year group has an online forum to keep people up to date with what is going on in the school. Write an article explaining why your group has chosen this charity and encouraging students to get involved.

Plan your writing, and check and edit your writing so it is clear for your reader.

Write between 150 and 250 words.

You will be marked on:

- length: writing a minimum of 150 words
- ideas: providing information and details that are appropriate for your audience and purpose
- structure: organising your ideas clearly and appropriately, with a clear beginning, middle and ending
- language choices: choosing words and sentences that are appropriate for your audience and purpose
- accuracy: using correct spelling, punctuation and grammar.

PLANNING

Who is my audience? ______________________________

What is my purpose? ______________________________

Remember all the advice about planning and structuring an article (pages 82–85).

THINK: what do I know about this topic?

 ISBN: 9780170477581

TIME TO WRITE

CHECK YOUR WORK

- Have I got names from the question right?
- Is it long enough?
- Is it organised into paragraphs?
- Is there a capital letter at the start of every sentence?
- Is there a full stop at the end of every sentence?
- Is my spelling okay? Have I used any available spellchecker?
- Does it say all I want to say on the topic?

If you are writing by hand, you may have to add extra refill pages. If you are typing your writing on a computer rather than in this book, then printing the page is a good idea.

QUESTION 5

You have been asked to write a short article for the advice column in your school's brochure for new students. Choose one of the following topics and give some good advice to a student arriving next year. You could offer personal anecdotes and practical tips.

- **Making friends**
- **Handling academic pressure**
- **Participating in extra-curricular activities**
- **Managing time effectively tricky?**
- **Surviving the first day**
- **Finding your way around**

Plan your writing, and check and edit your writing so it is clear for your reader.

Write between 150 and 250 words.

You will be marked on:

- length: writing a minimum of 150 words
- ideas: providing information and details that are appropriate for your audience and purpose
- structure: organising your ideas clearly and appropriately, with a clear beginning, middle and ending
- language choices: choosing words and sentences that are appropriate for your audience and purpose
- accuracy: using correct spelling, punctuation and grammar.

PLANNING

Who is my audience? ______________________________

What is my purpose? ______________________________

Remember all the advice about planning and structuring an article (pages 82–85).

THINK: what do I know about this topic?

 ISBN: 9780170477581

TIME TO WRITE

If you are writing by hand, you may have to add extra refill pages. If you are typing your writing on a computer rather than in this book, then printing the page is a good idea.

CHECK YOUR WORK

- Have I got names from the question right?
- Is it long enough?
- Is it organised into paragraphs?
- Is there a capital letter at the start of every sentence?
- Is there a full stop at the end of every sentence?
- Is my spelling okay? Have I used any available spellchecker?
- Does it say all I want to say on the topic?

QUESTION 6

Your school is running an International Festival and wants to invite several local cultural groups to perform. You have been given the task of writing an email to Atamai Latu, who used to go to your school and is a member of a Pacific Island performance group. Ask Atamai if he, and his group, would attend the International Festival.

Plan your writing, and check and edit your writing so it is clear for your reader.

Write between 150 and 250 words.

You will be marked on:

- length: writing a minimum of 150 words
- ideas: providing information and details that are appropriate for your audience and purpose
- structure: organising your ideas clearly and appropriately, with a clear beginning, middle and ending
- language choices: choosing words and sentences that are appropriate for your audience and purpose
- accuracy: using correct spelling, punctuation and grammar.

PLANNING

Who is my audience? ______________________________

What is my purpose? ______________________________

Remember all the advice about planning and structuring an email (page 75).

THINK: what do I know about this topic?

 ISBN: 9780170477581

TIME TO WRITE

CHECK YOUR WORK

- Have I got names from the question right?
- Is it long enough?
- Is it organised into paragraphs?
- Is there a capital letter at the start of every sentence?
- Is there a full stop at the end of every sentence?
- Is my spelling okay? Have I used any available spellchecker?
- Does it say all I want to say on the topic?

If you are writing by hand, you may have to add extra refill pages. If you are typing your writing on a computer rather than in this book, then printing the page is a good idea.

QUESTION 7

You were on the organising committee for your school Careers Expo. You have been asked to write a newsletter article for the parents of the students at your school, describing how valuable an experience the expo was for those that attended.

Plan your writing, and check and edit your writing so it is clear for your reader.

Write between 150 and 250 words.

You will be marked on:

- length: writing a minimum of 150 words
- ideas: providing information and details that are appropriate for your audience and purpose
- structure: organising your ideas clearly and appropriately, with a clear beginning, middle and ending
- language choices: choosing words and sentences that are appropriate for your audience and purpose
- accuracy: using correct spelling, punctuation and grammar.

PLANNING

Who is my audience? ______________________________

What is my purpose? ______________________________

Remember all the advice about planning and structuring an article (pages 82–85).

THINK: what do I know about this topic?

 ISBN: 9780170477581

TIME TO WRITE

If you are writing by hand, you may have to add extra refill pages. If you are typing your writing on a computer rather than in this book, then printing the page is a good idea.

CHECK YOUR WORK

- Have I got names from the question right?
- Is it long enough?
- Is it organised into paragraphs?
- Is there a capital letter at the start of every sentence?
- Is there a full stop at the end of every sentence?
- Is my spelling okay? Have I used any available spellchecker?
- Does it say all I want to say on the topic?

ISBN: 9780170477581

QUESTION 8

Write an article for the end-of-year school magazine for a group that you have been involved in this year. It should review/explain/share your achievements.

It could be a:

- **sports team**
- **performing arts group**
- **extra-curricular club (Robotics, Debating, Chess, ...)**
- **prefects/house captains**
- **community service (library, canteen, Breakfast Club, After School Club for juniors, ...).**

Plan your writing, and check and edit your writing so it is clear for your reader.

Write between 250 and 350 words.

You will be marked on:

- length: writing a minimum of 250 words
- ideas: providing information and details that are appropriate for your audience and purpose
- structure: organising your ideas clearly and appropriately, with a clear beginning, middle and ending
- language choices: choosing words and sentences that are appropriate for your audience and purpose
- accuracy: using correct spelling, punctuation and grammar.

PLANNING

Who is my audience? ______________________________

What is my purpose? ______________________________

Remember all the advice about planning and structuring an article (pages 82–85).

THINK: what do I know about this topic?

 ISBN: 9780170477581

TIME TO WRITE

CHECK YOUR WORK

- Have I got names from the question right?
- Is it long enough?
- Is it organised into paragraphs?
- Is there a capital letter at the start of every sentence?
- Is there a full stop at the end of every sentence?
- Is my spelling okay? Have I used any available spellchecker?
- Does it say all I want to say on the topic?

If you are writing by hand, you may have to add extra refill pages. If you are typing your writing on a computer rather than in this book, then printing the page is a good idea.

 ISBN: 9780170477581

QUESTION 9

Your school is planning an exchange trip with a school in a different country (choose the country yourself). You think it would be a fantastic experience. Write an email to the organising committee explaining why you think this is a good choice of destination and why you would really like to be included in the trip.

Plan your writing, and check and edit your writing so it is clear for your reader.

Write between 250 and 350 words.

You will be marked on:

- length: writing a minimum of 250 words
- ideas: providing information and details that are appropriate for your audience and purpose
- structure: organising your ideas clearly and appropriately, with a clear beginning, middle and ending
- language choices: choosing words and sentences that are appropriate for your audience and purpose
- accuracy: using correct spelling, punctuation and grammar.

PLANNING

Who is my audience? ______________________________

What is my purpose? ______________________________

Remember all the advice about planning and structuring an email (page 75).

THINK: what do I know about this topic?

TIME TO WRITE

ISBN: 9780170477581

If you are writing by hand, you may have to add extra refill pages. If you are typing your writing on a computer rather than in this book, then printing the page is a good idea.

CHECK YOUR WORK

- Have I got names from the question right?
- Is it long enough?
- Is it organised into paragraphs?
- Is there a capital letter at the start of every sentence?
- Is there a full stop at the end of every sentence?
- Is my spelling okay? Have I used any available spellchecker?
- Does it say all I want to say on the topic?

Answers

Answers start on page 120. You will also note that the answers are upside down. This is to hinder any easy copying of answers. After all, they won't be available in the assessment, so it is important that you develop your own skills.

2 My brother, who is the hungriest person in the world, just loves hamburgers.
3 Every week, at half past six on a Sunday morning, I get up, put on my running shoes and go for a 10-kilometre run.
4 'I'm going to feed the chooks,' said Janet.
5 Chop up vegetables (peppers, carrots, celery) and toss them into your favourite chilli recipe. If you don't like vegetables much, sneak them into foods you do enjoy (like grating carrots into tomato sauce or, again, courgettes into bread). It's a great way to get your veggies without having to taste them!

Speech marks ('…') (pages 46–47)

1 'It's six o'clock and here's the latest news,' burbled the radio.
'Sitiveni, where are you?' yelled Mum.
'Here,' he whispered. 'Shh, don't bark,' he said to the dog.
'A tornado has struck up north …' the radio droned on.
2 When I was younger, my favourite book was 'The Twits' by Roald Dahl. I particularly liked the chapter called 'The Great Upside Down Monkey Circus'.
3 'I solemnly swear that I am up to no good' is said by Harry Potter when he wants to use the Marauder's Map.

Apostrophe (') (pages 47–48)

1 Six children's coats were left on the school bus, but the driver didn't want to look after them.
2 Huan's favourite subject is Geography because he's a whizz at drawing maps.
3 It should've rained today, but instead the sun's heat was intense.
4 It's easy to talk about getting fit, but it's not easy to do it!
5 Ariki can't find his footy kit because I've hidden it in the shed.

SENTENCES — THE BASICS

What is a conjunction? (page 51)

1 Sione waited for the train, **but** it was running late **so** he knew he'd miss soccer practice.
2 We needed a place to study **so** we went to the library **because** it was quiet there.
3 **Although** I asked for a lemon ice block, the shopkeeper gave me an orange one.
4 Aroha whispered her question **while** we were in class **and** she got me in trouble.
5 I'm wearing a woolly jersey **yet** I'm still cold.

and … and … and … (page 52)

1 Whakapapa is a brilliant place to go for skiing and snowboarding. You can stay nearby at National Park, but we stay at Ohakune. My aunt has a place there that we can use. We drive over to Whakapapa every day to ski.
2 I love to play basketball. I'm allowed to play each night for an hour outside the garage at home. I would play all day, every day if I could. My sister shoots hoops with me.
3 Orienteering is a great way to keep fit and to learn navigation skills. Anyone can join a club. We start on white courses because they are the easiest. Then the yellow, orange and red courses get harder, but clubs help people to learn.

Tenses — the basics (page 53)

1 I ate my dinner at a café yesterday.
2 Huan drove to school in his mum's car yesterday.
3 Mieke chose a new dress yesterday.
4 They knew their results yesterday.

5 I said to my teddy that we went to the mall yesterday. We brought back some new paints. Then I drew a picture of him when he fell off the shelf. After that, we ate dinner and he slept in my bed.

SPELLING — THE BASICS

Homophones (page 54)

1 site — 2 write
3 maid/made — 4 knew/new
5 hole/whole — 6 it's/its

Practice set 1 (page 56)

1 B — 2 D
3 A — 4 B
5 B — 6 D
7 C — 8 C, A, B, D

Practice set 2 (page 57)

1 D — 2 A
3 B — 4 B
5 A — 6 B
7 D, B, A, C — 8 A

Practice set 3 (page 58)

1 D — 2 B
3 C — 4 C
5 A — 6 D
7 B — 8 A

Practice set 4 (page 59)

1 A — 2 C
3 B — 4 B
5 C — 6 D
7 C — 8 B

Practice set 5 (page 60)

1 C — 2 C
3 C — 4 B
5 C — 6 C, B, A, D
7 A — 8 B

Practice set 6 (page 61)

1 C — 2 B
3 D — 4 B
5 D — 6 C
7 D — 8 A

Practice set 7 (page 62)

1 D — 2 B
3 C — 4 B
5 B — 6 A
7 C — 8 D

Let's get writing

It's difficult to assess your own writing. If these writing tasks are being done through school, a teacher will check your writing for you as part of your preparation for the Literacy Writing assessment.

If you are doing the writing tasks independently, politely ask a teacher or someone else who you know is good with words to read what you have written and give you feedback on how well you have communicated your ideas.

Always complete you own check first by reading the finished piece through with critical eyes.

ISBN: 9780170477581

ISBN: 9780170477581

Text 8: Cook Strait curse (pages 24–25)

1 B **2** A
3 D **4** C
5 C
6 There is absolutely no way that he can get a sailing any earlier.
7 The article mentions a curse ... it is the latest in an ongoing saga for Cook Strait ferries, which have been dogged by multiple breakdowns and weather-related cancellations. A curse is something that causes things to go wrong time and time again no matter what you do. It seems that this is the case for Bluebridge.
8 Answers will vary, but should include: to prove that the article is researched, to show different perspectives and how this has affected the passengers and that the management is aware of the issue.
9 Both the ferry company and people/travellers trying to cross the Strait.
10 Answers will vary, but could include: potential travellers, people who live in the area (published in *Marlborough Midweek*).

Text 9: Chatham honey tours (pages 26–27)

1 D **2** A
3 B **4** D
5 B
6 Suggested: to show that the tour won't only showcase the honey bees; that the weeklong tour of the Chatham Islands will give the participant a full experience of the Chatham Islands.
7 To show that the company is using new features/techniques/skills to create products and/or to let us know it is something new on the market.
8 About 200.
9 Commercial operators work on a large scale and sell the product for profit/gain. Hobbyists are not professional. They have beehives to enjoy the process, help the bees and enjoy honey if they can.
10 Answers will vary, but will likely mention that these are the summary parts of the article and who to contact for more information — these two bits are made to stand out in case you don't have time to read the whole article.

Text 10: Your dog: kibble vs raw feeding (pages 28–29)

1 A **2** B
3 D **4** C
5 A
6 So that we can see things from others' perspectives and get a balanced and educated view before making our own choices.
7 That it is important because each feeding option has its own advantages and disadvantages, and it ultimately depends on the individual dog's needs and the owner's preferences.
8 For: natural, correct nutrients, no fillers, no artificial preservatives.
Against: can be dangerous, expensive, time consuming, bacteria, unbalanced, needs care to prepare.
9 They care deeply for their pets; the topic has conflicting information and marketing, which can lead to confusion and different opinions.
10 The conversation highlights that different feeding options come with different costs and time commitments, and that owners need to consider their own lifestyle and budget when making a decision. Table reinforces these ideas.

Text 11: School embraces RecycleKiwi (pages 30–31)

1 A **2** C
3 C **4** D
5 C **6** B

Text 12: The Perfect Ring (pages 32–33)

1 B **2** D
3 D **4** D
5 B

Text 13: Kura M⊠ori empowering next generation (pages 34–35)

1 B **2** D
3 A **4** C
5 D

Text 14: A career highlight (pages 36–37)

1 A **2** D
3 B **4** D
5 C

Text 15: Science on the Ice (pages 38–39)

1 D **2** C
3 B **4** A
5 A **6** D

Text 16: Wildboy (pages 40–41)

1 C **2** B
3 A **4** A
5 D **6** D

Let's be accurate

PUNCTUATION — THE BASICS

The capital letter (page 43)

1 In April, my family is going to Brisbane to see our cousin Wiremu.
2 Jack and Jill went up to Auckland to see ***Battle of the Teen Bands***.
3 My sister eats an apple every day, but I hate apples.
4 I hope I get a bike for my birthday because my old one is useless.
5 We're flying to Samoa for Christmas to stay with family in Apia.

The full stop (.) (page 44)

1 There is a park at the end of my street. I go there most weekends. If my friend Aroha is around she comes too.
2 My duvet is on the floor. My books are on the floor. My clothes are on the floor. I get called untidy. I don't know why.
3 ⊠taki is an area with lots of attractions for visitors. ⊠taki has so much to see and do. It's a hidden gem in the greater Wellington region.
4 Mars is a cold desert world. It is half the size of Earth. Mars is sometimes called the Red Planet. It's red because of rusty iron in the ground.
5 To make Rocky Road bring a pot of water to the boil with a glass bowl on top. Gently melt the chocolate in the bowl, stirring constantly. Remove once fully melted.

The question mark (?) (page 44)

1 May we go to the park, Mum?
2 Everyone asks me if I'm going in the talent competition. (No question mark required)
3 You don't like coffee, do you?
4 If it's raining, how come the sun is shining?
5 'Can you send me the link?' asked Joe.

The exclamation mark (!) (page 45)

1 I am so scared! Will it hurt?
2 We'll be late, hurry up! You're so slow.
3 Is it much further?
4 That test was so easy! I wonder if I'll pass with flying colours?
5 Hey, budding astronomers, listen up. How well do you know your own solar system? Can you put the planets in the proper order? This interactive game helps students to sort out the planets and it's fun!

The comma (,) (page 46)

1 Sunita went to the shop to buy streamers, balloons, candles, party poppers and a cake for the birthday party.

 ISBN: 9780170477581

Answers

Answers written in response to the short answer questions will not be the same for every student. Your answers may not be exactly the same as the sample answers we offer in the book. You might compare your answer with a friend's answer to check your reasoning…and theirs. If you need help, just politely ask a teacher to check for you.

Let's get reading

Pages 7 and 8

1 B
2 A

Text 1: Tracking from *The Reluctant Hero* (pages 10–11)

1 A
2 D
3 B
4 B
5 D
6 Because the target audience is predominantly New Zealand males. A lot of New Zealand males go hunting, so Apiata is bringing in something familiar for the audience so they can better understand his point.
7 That you leave even more signs for the people tracking you, making you easier to see.
8 That the clues left will allow the tracker to fill in the blanks and tell you what (most likely) happened.
9 Because 'poo' is informal language and although this is a story, it is still for publication and words should be given their proper term.
10 Answers will vary, but could include observation/looking carefully at things.

Text 2: Ride like your aunty is watching (pages 12–13)

1 C
2 C
3 B
4 D
5 D
6 That the illustrations are designed in a way that is easy to understand and that they show common scenarios and behaviours that passengers may encounter or exhibit while using Metlink's services.
7 It is a transport agency in New Zealand that co-ordinates transport across trains, buses and ferries.
8 Passengers and potential passengers.
9 Answers will vary, but should include adults and younger children (see images).
10 Answers will vary, but should include that a teenager is depicted as the main character.

Text 3: The Underwater Classroom (pages 14–15)

1 D
2 A
3 B
4 C
5 A
6 Answers will vary, but should or will refer to education in some way.
7 Because it gave them a chance to see how animals behave differently at different times (i.e. night).
8 Answers will vary, but should will include danger.
9 Someone touched the jellyfish and didn't get stung.
10 'We learnt more in a short time through actual experiences than using books and the internet.' (Last line of text.)

Text 4: North Island: A Volcanic Heritage (pages 16–17)

1 C
2 B
3 D
4 B
5 D
6 Because the way the land is shaped, with ridges, hills, deep gullies and ravines, looks similar to how a large fish would look after being hacked at with a knife (rather than being eaten cleanly). It suggests that the spine of the fish (now the highlands) has been exposed.
7 It isn't clear until the end, but the writer is making a point that the North Island of New Zealand has been shaped by volcanic forces, which are still active today.
8 Any positive words, e.g. *spectacular, ecstatic, sheer, awesomely.*
9 The volcanic activity (clue is in the title). Could mention 'violent (volcanic) explosions' and also 'sulphurous breath'.
10 The author thinks it is mysterious how similar the outline of the North Island is to a fish, considering the M⊠ori didn't have maps as we do and could not see such a long coastline as a complete shape.

Text 5: Reviews of the novel *The Bone Tiki* (pages 18–19)

1 D
2 B
3 D
4 A
5 A
6 Ramesh. The review is 100% positive, but doesn't really give any specific details about the book. It could be a generic review applied to any book.
7 Answers will vary. Suggestions: holds the reader's attention, keeps the reader interested.
8 Because she quotes the main character, saying 'I also "learned things about my own culture I didn't even know"' and links it to herself, implying she is M⊠ori, too.
9 The speed that the storyline moves.
10 Answers will vary, but might mention: to attract readers, to build up hype for the book, to make their review stand out. Descriptive language can help readers visualise the book, help convey the reviewer's opinion quickly.

Text 6: Settlement Opinion (pages 20–21)

1 D
2 D
3 A
4 B
5 A
6 Answers will vary, but may include: because each situation is different, different experience in the past with the Crown, different groups of people involved, …
7 Answers will vary. Male/female/ younger/older, different tribes, no P⊠keh⊠.
8 Matahana Tikao Calman: te reo M⊠ori, tutoring scholarships Tui: saving, fees paid, strong local economy.
9 Answers will vary, but must include reasoning. Teneti Ririnui followed it closely.
10 Answers will vary, but should touch on hearing different perspectives, consider different viewpoints and then to form their own opinions.

Text 7: Mussel Building (pages 22–23)

1 C
2 B
3 D
4 A
5 C
6 The language used is te reo M⊠ori, native to New Zealand: Kura, ⊠hiwa, p⊠tangaroa ('a native species').
7 The iwi had noticed and were concerned about the decline and want to work together to find out what has happened to the mussel beds.
8 The p⊠tangaroa are eating the mussels. Paul-Burke saw hundreds of thousands of p⊠tangaroa and behind them, empty green-lipped mussel shells. The team hung restoration stations out of reach of the p⊠tangaroa and the mussels thrived.
9 Because natural fibres are traditionally part of M⊠ori culture; plastic damages the environment; because natural fibres will break down naturally.
10 That the mussel beds are re-establishing and the mussel population had increased tenfold.